Ladies, Start Your Engines!!

by
Jan King

CCC PUBLICATIONS

Published by

CCC Publications
1111 Rancho Conejo Blvd.
Suites 411 & 412
Newbury Park, CA 91320

Manufactured in the United States of America

Cover © 1996 CCC Publications

Cover/Interior production by Oasis Graphics

ISBN: 1-57644-016-8

If your local U.S. bookstore is out of stock, copies of this book may be
obtained by mailing check or money order for $7.99 per book (plus $3.00
to cover postage and handling) to: CCC Publications; 1111 Rancho Conejo
Blvd.; Suites 411 & 412; Newbury Park, CA 91320

Pre-publication Edition – 6/96

Dedication

To my dear friend Ray E. Friedman
who is loved by all for the great humanitarian he is

And in loving memory of the late
Evelyn R. Friedman
whose love lives on through all who knew her

TABLE OF CONTENTS

INTRODUCTION

Has the passion gone out of your relationship like the bubbles out of stale champagne? It seems like one minute it's very effervescent and then the next thing you know, those little bubbles have all evaporated into thin air. It's not that it has turned *sour*, it's just *flat*. Wouldn't you like to get those exciting *bubbles* back into your relationship? Well, you can. "Ladies, Start Your Engines" is going to give you insights and techniques you can use to reignite the fires of romance and passion you experienced when you and your partner were beginning your relationship.

I have interviewed about one thousand men and women from all walks of life in person and through questionnaires on this topic. The book contains many direct quotes from these women concerning their marital and relationship problems. It also contains some excellent advice from those women who have been successful in keeping the sizzle in their marriages. Most of the women in this book are in marriages which are by no means close to divorce, but they are suffering from a lack of passion and experiencing sexual apathy. Many of the women have said that *although they still "love" their husbands, they don't have the feeling of being "in love" with them like they used to.*

There are many people who feel its a given that after three or more years of marriage, the romance and passion HAS TO cool off significantly. Most accept this as an inevitable part of life. But this doesn't have to be the case. And furthermore, if you accept this theory of diminishing passion and romance over the course of time, it's EVENTUALLY GOING TO HAPPEN in your own relationship. *There ARE marriages that get stronger, more passionate and the sex gets better and better over the years*. The goal of this book is to have YOUR marriage or relationship become as romantically and sexually fulfilling as one of these.

I am also speaking to you in this book from my own personal experience. I have personally been through the trauma of divorce, and it's given me a much greater understanding and perspective of the pitfalls in relationships. Happily, I have been remarried for four and a half blissful years. And believe me, in this marriage, I am practicing all the advice I'm dispensing to you! AND IT WORKS! People always think my husband and I are newlyweds, because we still have that electric chemistry in our personal interactions. So I am telling you firsthand–passion and romance are entirely possible to keep in your relationship as long as you *make it your priority*.

We will be exploring how negative communication can lead to built-up resentment which squeezes the sex and passion out of relationships over time. We will talk about this in chapters dealing with arguments, children, sexual image, trust, respect, jealousy and many other related subjects. It is never one factor which acts to diminish love and passion in a relationship, rather, a combination of problems all relating to the topics mentioned above. *And the thread which ties all of it together is COMMUNICATION.* It is vital to discover how and why your communication is or isn't working for you in attempting to keep your relationship a nurturing and passionate one.

Now, we all recognize that in order for a relationship to grow it takes the commitment and work of both people in it. *But always remember, you can only control one half of every relationship you're in–your half.* Therefore, this book is suggesting that you the woman, swallow your pride and be the one who takes the first step towards reviving the passion in your marriage or relationship. I have written this book from a woman's point of view, taking the attitude that a woman can't keep waiting around *forever* for her husband to *get the message.* You will be old and gray before that happens! So you are going to have to take the *bull by the horns* and start the revitalization process. However, I have included a CUT–OUT SECTION at the end of the book JUST FOR THE MEN which gives them insights and advice about how *they* can help you in your quest to put the SIZZLE back in your relationship. Naturally, I had to bribe them a bit by promising them that you are working towards becoming more "sexual and sensual" for them. You are going to have a lot of FUN in the process of re-discovering your sexuality and stirring up those dormant passions. And your mates are going to LOVE the *new you* and the SEXUAL SPICINESS you'll infuse into your relationship!

CHAPTER 1

HOW IT WAS

WHAT WE LOST

Remember the excitement we felt when we were first dating our husbands? Remember that incredible passion we felt as our hearts thumped in our chests over the excitement of his voice, his touch or his kiss?

Most of the married women or women in long-term relationships I interviewed are troubled by the fact that those *romantic feelings* are simply not there or expressed anymore. Although they feel their marriages are sound, they can't help but feel a twinge of jealousy when they see couples who are openly affectionate and radiate those passionate sparks long gone from their own relationships.

Many women said that after two or three years of marriage, their relationships could be described as "comfortable," "functional," "routine" or in some cases even "boring." While most affirmed that they did indeed still love their husbands, they felt that the sensation of being "in love" had evaporated. Their sex had become "routine" rather than "passionate." They began noticing a lot more "flaws" in their mates and instead of doing things together as they once did, they were finding interests separate from their spouses. They got into activities involving their kids or developed a passion for sports, like playing tennis. The things that now occupied their time didn't include their husbands.

WHY DID WE LOSE IT?

So why does this happen? Is it just *one* or a *combination* of circumstances that puts an emotional damper on our relationships– cooling down the passion and causing some emotional distancing? Or is it just an inevitable fact of life that none of us will be able to avoid? Most women choose the latter for an explanation. They say it's *normal* that after having been married for a number of years the passion in any relationship is bound to *cool off.*

I totally disagree with this way of thinking because I have also interviewed *many women* whose relationships are as hot as ever after years of marriage. It has not been impossible for them to keep the passion flowing after years of being together. But it takes commitment and the willingness to practice certain techniques and behaviors we will talk in-depth about in this book. I hate using the phrase "working at it" because it tends to conjure up thoughts of doing things that involve drudgery and aren't fun. But this isn't so. Some of the things involve *will power and commitment*– like changing the way you argue with your spouse. Others are really fun–like *planning dates with your husband* and *scheduling alone time* with him.

But in order to fully understand the paths which have led to this emotional cooling, you'll have to go back and remember in detail the things you did which made your new relationship so passionate. I have taken quotes from letters women have written to me and used them to preface each separate topic. We will use them to explore each subject, identifying those feelings and moments of passion we once shared with our partners.

THE EMOTIONAL CLIMATE

I think we would all agree that when we were dating we were all on our *best behavior*. So what does that actually mean? The following are topics women addressed when recounting the kinds of feelings and interactions that were vital ingredients of passionate relationships in their past.

♥♥♥"WE WERE ALWAYS SHOWING OUR LOVE OPENLY FOR ONE ANOTHER. WE COULDN'T DO ENOUGH FOR EACH OTHER. EVERYDAY WE WOULD EXCHANGE LOVE NOTES, LITTLE GIFTS, AND STUFF LIKE THAT."

> **Shared acts which demonstrate a couples' love for one another and making each other a priority are all part of nurturing the relationship.**

♥NURTURING EACH OTHER AND THE RELATIONSHIP–This is one of the first things that comes to womens' minds when we remember how it was when we were in the passionate stages of actively pursuing one another. What all these *new beginnings* have in common is that both parties put forth an ONGOING EFFORT to show how deeply they care for each another. It is behavior which comes straight from the heart and is translated into showing KINDNESS TO EACH OTHER in every way possible. We experienced it when our men opened the doors for us, pulled our chairs out for us, helped us on with our coats, bought us little gifts, left love notes on our pillows, sent flowers and thought up a hundred other thoughtful ways of showing how much they loved us. And it was done on a daily basis! It was also common-place to say "thank you" or "I love you" to each other for the little things we did or acknowledge the other's kindness by saying "that means a lot to me." Couples who are actively in the process of winning each other's hearts spend time asking the other about themselves, com-plimenting each other and showing mutual support for everything they do. This is what we refer to as "nurturing" each other.

When we were receiving this kind of affirmation on a daily basis, women found it easy to reciprocate. We showed an active interest in his work, we attended sporting events with him, we cooked him special din-ners, sent him cards and love notes, called him several times a day, helped him on with his jacket and dressed to please him. We were careful to be on time, act cheerfully and eager to win his approval in every facet of the rela-tionship. Both parties performed hundreds of endearing acts in a natural and unbegrudging way. It was easy. When you're madly in love with some-one, it's perfectly natural to do everything you can to make him happy. And do you know what? An interesting thing happened. We found that THE MORE WE GAVE, THE MORE WE GOT IN RETURN in terms of uncon-ditional love and support.

"WE WOULD SPEND HOURS TALKING ABOUT OURSELVES–OUR HOPES AND DREAMS AND WHAT WE WANTED OUT OF LIFE. WE NEVER SEEMED TO RUN OUT OF THINGS TO TALK ABOUT. WE WERE EACH OTHER'S BEST FRIEND AS WELL AS LOVERS."

> **This is what is known as an honest and open two-way commu-nication. It is borne out of true passion for each other and is what allows bonding and intimacy to occur.**

♥COMPLETE COMMUNICATION–Dating is an exciting time of exploring who the other person is and finding out everything about them we can. And to accomplish that, we need to communicate on a very intense level. Couples spend a majority of their time and effort in finding out about the other person's likes and dislikes in every imag-inable area. They spend hours discussing their families, their child-hoods, their hopes and dreams and what would make them happy in the future. They find out what kind of books, movies, sports, foods, clothes and hundreds of other things they like. Both are extremely interested in each other's present values and goals for the future. *Talking is really easy at this point of the relationship.*

In a *new love* situation, both parties spend hours *talking about their relationship with each other*. They verbalize exactly what it is about the other person they love, how they love sharing that love and all facets of the bonding which is taking place between them. In this way, the relationship itself becomes an unending source of communication and couples devote much of their time and energies to nurturing it. Couples who are newly in love would rather spend their time alone talking with each other than surrounded by distracting groups of people. They don't need the conversations of others to keep things interesting and fill in the voids because there are none. They don't want other people around them taking away their time together because it is so important to them. *They don't need other people to have fun.* They are able to completely fulfill each other in every way.

♥♥♥"WE ALWAYS HAD THE BEST TIMES TOGETHER. WE HAD A BALL DOING THINGS LIKE ROLLER SKATING, GOING ON PICNICS AND MAKING LOVE ON THE BEACH AT TWO O'CLOCK IN THE MORNING."

> **The closeness present in the beginning of intense relationships keeps both parties secure, happy and fun-loving. They are always searching for exciting and creative things to do with each other.**

♥CREATING PLAYTIME TOGETHER–Dating means *doing* rather than *being*. Dating couples make it a priority to "have fun" together and create really enjoyable playtime for themselves. Besides going to the movies or out to dinner, dating couples experience the fun of going dancing, making picnics, skiing, going to the theater, going to art galleries and attending lots of parties. They experiment with the so-called "in things" to do like roller blading, sailing, line-dancing and flea-marketing. Dating couples seem to have limitless energy to meet after work for drinks and dinner, go camping on the weekends or engage in any number of one-on-one activities.

Many women said that during the height of the passionate period of their relationships, they were never at a loss for interesting things to do with their mates. One woman said she and her fiancee always made a joyous event out of a "nothing afternoon" by "walking in the snow" or "trying on crazy hats in a department store" or "toasting marshmallows in their apartment fireplace." "We were always willing to be a part of the other's plans and had fun sharing everything from cooking dinner together to washing each other's hair."

♥"WE WOULD RATHER BE WITH EACH OTHER THAN WITH ANY-ONE ELSE IN THE WORLD. WE PUT EACH OTHER FIRST IN EVERY ASPECT OF OUR LIVES."

This is what is known as making your loved one the #1 priority in your life.

♥MAKING EACH OTHER A PRIORITY–In most instances, *couples who are passionately involved with each other make the other person their whole world.* They never find it too difficult or inconvenient to reschedule work or family obligations to spend time with each other. The men will not mind giving up some of their usual sporting events, poker games or other male-oriented activities in favor of spending time with their women. And vice-versa. The gals make a valiant effort to be dressed and ready on time, cut back their girl talk on the phone, give up a night out with the girls and in general, rearrange their lives to be with their guy. Both parties really *want* to do it for them. It's no sacrifice to rearrange their lives and make their loved one come first in terms of their time and interest. They just can't see enough of each other. And by doing this, a very powerful trust is built between the parties. They know that they can count on each other 100% for anything and that the other person will *be there for them* without fail.

This kind of positive reinforcement lets the other person know how much they are loved on a continuing basis. In one of the many letters I received, a woman put it this way: "There was never any question as to where I stood in the relationship. I was adored– and not just by words alone. His way of putting me first made me feel loved and totally secure. I loved him so much for doing that and showed him by treating him the same way."

♥"HE WAS SO PATIENT WITH ME. IF I MESSED SOMETHING UP LIKE BEING LATE OR MAKING A MISTAKE, I NEVER FEARED A REPRISAL LIKE BEING CALLED STUPID. HE TREATED ME WITH LOVE AND KINDNESS AND ALWAYS FOUND TIME TO GIVE ME THE HELP AND SUPPORT I NEEDED."

> Time has no limits for those who are passionately in love. They always make it for each other in their sustained effort to show the depth of their love. They do it by showing a great deal of patience for each other.

♥PATIENCE AND UNDERSTANDING–We could all take a lesson from the patience expressed by loving couples in their treatment of one another. If there ever was a time when we made allowances, it was when we were first deeply involved with our mates. Women said they remember how happy they were doing things for their loved ones they normally wouldn't have had a big interest in–like attending a sporting event. They did it to *please* their man. And likewise, their men would tag along for hours of shopping on a Saturday afternoon–a time when they normally would have been ensconced in front of the tube watching football or out playing sports. If one of them became ill the other would do whatever it took to nurse the other back to health. The guys would show infinite patience in teaching the women how to drive a stick shift or teaching them the rules of a sport like baseball. Women also said they used to spend much of their time with their mates exchanging ideas on topics from child rearing to politics so they could be more of one mind on important issues.

Passionate couples have a way of overlooking the human frailties of the other and dwelling on the positive. One woman said that it seemed like they never "criticized or found fault with each other." Another said, "If there were things about the other we weren't crazy about, we took the time to try and understand them so we could cope better." It is true that people who are *madly in love* become quite adept at defending each other's faults to the rest of the world. And this takes a great deal of patience and understanding. Some refer to this behavior by saying "love is blind." But whatever you call it, the fact is that these couples demonstrate their depth of love by the total acceptance of the other. *They always seek to find the good in the other person and do not get stuck dwelling in the negative.*

♥♥♥"I WAS NEVER TREATED WITH SO MUCH KINDNESS AS WHEN MY HUSBAND AND I WERE FIRST MARRIED. HE WAS COMPLETELY FOCUSED ON MY NEEDS AND FEELINGS. I TRUSTED HIM COMPLETELY, BECAUSE I KNEW HE WOULD RATHER DIE THAN EVER HURT ME."

> **This statement shows us that when one person extends his kindness and love to another it will allow a deep trust to develop between them.**

♥KINDNESS—*Couples who are deeply involved go out of their way to show kindness and tenderness to the other.* A woman related this incident to me as an example of how her husband's kindness kept them passionate and connected.

One woman told how her husband's unfaltering support during a difficult time kept them extremely bonded emotionally. "I was going through a very tough period early on in our marriage because my mother became terminally ill. I spent a lot of time taking care of her during the day and would come home emotionally and physically exhausted at night. My husband always encouraged me to get my feelings out and would hold my hand while I cried endlessly. He never complained about being neglected himself and supported me through it all with tenderness and empathy. The kind of feeling I had for him was the deepest love for another human being that anyone could ever experience. We were completely bonded emotionally and physically. No matter how tired I was, I looked forward to lying in his arms and making love with him. It was a time when I never felt so loved or so loving in all my life."

Another woman put it succinctly: "When someone is treating you kindly, you can't help but give it back in return." How true for all of us. Kindness is a direct expression of love. Showing tenderness and kindness are acts which have a far more permanent effect than any words which can be said. And those who are deeply in love will also extend that same kindness to the people their loved ones care about. For example, this woman wrote about the early days of her relationship with the man she later married: "He was not only kind to me but to my parents, our friends and everyone else I cared about. He wanted everyone around us to be as happy as we were."

♥"WOW! WHO COULD FORGET THOSE DAYS WHEN WE MADE LOVE ALL NIGHT! I DON'T KNOW WHY, BUT WE NEVER GOT TIRED. WE JUST COULDN'T GET ENOUGH OF EACH OTHER. EACH TIME WAS MORE EXCITING THAN THE LAST!"

Often when we think of a new relationship, we think of fabulous, hot sex. And it's true in most cases. However, the sex is great BECAUSE the two people have got all the other factors we've talked about working for them in their relationship.

♥SEX AND INTIMACY–Assuming the couples are involved in a sexual relationship before marriage, there's a lot to discuss in this arena. In most of the cases presented to me in letters, the women said that the sex before marriage was when it was at it's most passionate. And gleaning from what the women wrote, there were several reasons for this.

– The Thrill Of Discovery

One of the most prevalent reasons for the couples' sex lives being so passionate before marriage was because their communication was operating at a very high level. They were interested in learning everything they could about each other emotionally as well as physically. The *newness* of their relationship provided that big bonus. It was a time when each person was so involved in the thrill of learning about each other, that each gave generously of himself in order to build up the other's self-esteem. And this *stroking* built a great deal of trust as well as generated a lot of passion between the two. And with this momentum going for them, they became more and more uninhibited with one another in the process of discovery. Sex became a very large part of the discovery process and therefore became a priority in their relationship. This passage from a middle-aged woman who wrote to me exemplifies the feelings of many other women I've talked to:

"Every time we made love, I learned something new about him that I adored. The smell of his neck, the sensitive parts of his body, the way he told me he loved me–everything became such a marvelous turn on."

And from another: "We spent hours caressing and holding each other. Sometimes we'd talk until the sun came up. I never felt so in-tune with another human being in my life. There wasn't a thing in our lovemaking I wasn't willing to do. We were so incredibly free of fear and mistrust."

–Women reported that in the early days of the relationship they were much more involved in experimenting sexually with the man they loved. They remembered their patience and eagerness to learn about the other and how it pleased them both. Both sides put forth an enormous effort to keep the relationship growing.

One woman said: "I couldn't believe my own sexual responsiveness. Sexual things that I had always feared might be distasteful to me, I found thrilling. I loved having oral sex with him and found myself incredibly aroused by anything he did. I trusted him completely."

All the women felt that these positive attitudes became self–perpetuating, heightening the passion in their relationships even more.

– The Individuals Saw Themselves As Sexual People

More than any other time, the women said they began to think of themselves as real *sexual* beings. They would go out and buy lacy teddies and other sexy lingerie, worked on their bodies in terms of diet and exercise and really enjoyed their status as being sexy in the eyes of their beloved. And it was constantly reinforced by the compliments they received from their men.

A woman from the South wrote about how she felt when she and her husband were engaged: "He was always telling me how gorgeous my breasts looked and how great my body felt to him. Not a day went by when he didn't make me feel like I was 'Miss America' or somebody equal to her. I absolutely ate it up. I never felt so good about myself or felt so sexy in my entire life."

And it worked both ways. The women also gave their men constant ego-boosts in this department. The men loved the fact that the women were trying so hard to please them and make themselves as sexually desirable as possible for them. Their behavior was not only a compliment but a real turn-on for their men as well.

There was another young woman who had this to say: "My boyfriend used to tell me what a turn-on it was that I kept myself in such good shape for him. He took it as a real compliment and said it boosted his ego more than anything else I did for him."

– Losing Their Inhibitions

From what I read, it was during the first two years of a relationship when women became the most sexually uninhibited. It's like anything else in life. The more you practice, the better you get. Women, especially, seemed to be at their most adventurous during the dating or engagement period. The couples had frequent sex in places like moonlit beaches, hotels and other places besides the conventional bedrooms. They were more open to oral sex, phone sex and other alternative ways of deriving pleasure. They seemed to be much more comfortable with their bodies than they were later on in their lives. In essence, there was simply a lot more willingness to explore each other as sexual human beings than at any other time in their lives.

A Mid-Western woman in her mid-thirties put it like this: "I used to love sex when my husband and I were first married before the kids came along. We had sex at least every day and more often twice a day. We used to make a point of doing it in a different room in the house each time, too. I can't believe how totally uninhibited we were. We'd make love in the

15

shower or on the kitchen floor–wherever and whenever the mood hit us! Even when I was dressed up to go out and he decided to 'attack' me I was always ready and willing. I didn't mind getting all mussed up one bit!"

– Openly Displaying Affection

Summing up the feelings of a new relationship vs. an old one, this woman put it succinctly: "Beginnings Are Beautiful."

When we observe how *new* couples interact, we would probably describe them as constantly being "all over each other." They openly demonstrate affectionate behavior such as hand holding, frequent kissing, playfully nibbling each others ears, constant touching, loving gazes and thousands of other things. These are all steps in the *physical bonding* process which can be observed between passionate couples. It is also referred to as having great *chemistry*. They are not embarrassed one bit to show their affection publicly. In fact, they are so "into each other" that most of them are completely unaware of anyone else around them.

A woman in her forties remembers it this way: "Those were the days when we only had eyes for each other. The entire world could be blowing up around us and we wouldn't have a clue. Our bonding was so strong that we could care less what other people thought of our behavior."

– The Desire To Learn More About Our Own Sexuality

During the time of passionate bonding between a couple, a woman's entire attitude about her own sexuality changes. It is no longer something to giggle about or to view equivocally. For passionate couples, sex becomes a priority in their lives. They are participants in something they find is making their relationship stronger. And because of the security this brings to the relationship, sex takes a priority and the couples want to perfect it. Women are more likely to seek out books which will teach them about the mechanics of sex, so they can learn the techniques and methods which will make them more orgasmic. They will seek advice and knowledge from girlfriends and other sources because they are in a willing mode to learn as much about sex as possible.

This young woman tells about her strong desire to learn more about her own sexuality:

"When we were in the first year of our relationship, I wanted to learn everything I could about sex to get more proficient at it. It was the glue that kept us emotionally and physically bonded 24 hours a day. I wanted him to think I was the best sexual partner he ever had. I really took it seriously. It was a huge part of our interaction."

Nowadays, there is a host of information available to both parties in terms of videotapes, books, movies, seminars and the like which couples can learn from. We live in an age where, fortunately, having frequent and fulfilling sex is no longer considered a shameful thing for women to pursue. Women have come into their own sexually now more than ever. Now, we're told it's O.K. to be sexually aggressive. Many men like that in women. We can ask for what we want in bed without being thought of as a "slut." Sex has become, thank heavens, no longer only a completely masculine domain.

THE ACTIVE INGREDIENTS

So far, we have discussed the different dynamics in new and growing relationships that are actively and regularly practiced. And we have seen how they contribute to making those new relationships so passionate and intense. During the process of forming a long-term commitment, both parties are WORKING ON and PRACTICING all the things we mentioned in this chapter on a lot of different levels. And when they see their relationships getting stronger because of it, the excitement generated keeps perpetuating these positive practices. As both parties build their relationship by discovering all they can about the other person, they put that knowledge into PRACTICE. Passion is dynamic. We are constantly creating and re-creating it in our relationships.

I think we'd all agree that if we put this much time and effort into our jobs and studies, we'd all be huge successes. And of course, many people do. But sadly when other concerns like our careers or other interests become a priority over the relationship, it's usually because we stopped practicing all those positive behaviors. *And when the relationship loses it's #1 status, its passion and intensity will definitely COOL OFF.*

This is what we will be exploring in the rest of the book. We will hear the opinions of women from all over the country about what they think contributed to the demise of the passion in their marriages and long-term relationships. We will explore the question of whether sex keeps the passion alive between couples or whether the passion has to be there FIRST in order to have fulfilling sex. We will look at how tenderness and kindness keep sex exciting and how trust is the basic ingredient underlying all of it. There will be theory as well as practical advice given by me and testimony from women all over the country just like yourself.

CHAPTER 2

HOW IT IS

WHAT IT'S LIKE NOW

The majority of women who shared their experiences with me had many thoughts in common. They were all in agreement that the passion and intimacy they once had earlier in their relationships had truly gone out of their marriages. Even though no single person's story duplicated the other, most of them said that sometime during the first five years of marriage, the strong passion and the frequency and intensity of sex with their spouses had dramatically cooled down.

However, there was a small percentage of women I talked with or who wrote to me whose experiences were quite different. Happily, the romance and passion in their relationships was as good or better than when they first dated their husbands. How they managed to keep their relationships cooking with passion will be discussed in a later chapter. What we will concern ourselves with now is the MAJORITY of women and what they said was happening in their relationships. And this accounted for about 90% of the women who wrote or personally gave me information for the book.

The majority of the women who reported that the romance and passion had died in their marriages also made a point of saying that they didn't feel their marriages were "bad" or "falling apart." But they did feel "emotionally isolated" from their husbands. Now, what exactly are we talking about when we use the term "passion?" It had different connotations for the people in various relationships whom I talked to. Some thought of it as a measure of the frequency and intensity of the sexual interaction with their partners. Others took the broader view of it encompassing all the emotional components of a relationship. This included feelings of excitement, affection, kindness, commitment and depth of feeling for their spouses. Let's take a look at the different yardsticks with which women measured the passion or lack of it in their relationships:

♥♥♥"IN THE FIRST TWO YEARS OF OUR MARRIAGE, WE HAD INTERCOURSE FIVE TO SEVEN TIMES A WEEK. IT WAS ALWAYS FULFILLING AND KEPT US VERY CLOSE EMOTIONALLY. NOW

AFTER FIFTEEN YEARS OF MARRIAGE, WE ONLY DO IT ABOUT ONCE OR TWICE A MONTH."

♥**Frequency of Intercourse**–There was a sharp discrepancy from an average of four to five times a week in the first few years of marriage down to an average of once or twice a week or less in some cases. Most of the women gave pretty much the same reasons for the decline in their frequency of lovemaking. One of them said, "It seems like just about everything gets in the way of our being able to have sex on a regular basis. Most of the time we're both exhausted from working all day at our jobs. At other times, some crisis occurred which used up all our emotional energy and dulled our sexual appetites. I hate to admit this but when we get into bed at night, I'd rather relax by reading a good book or watching TV. I just don't seem to have that burning desire for sex like I used to."

Another said, "It's like the less we do it, the less we want to do it. I feel kind of awkward about having sex anymore. I don't know why, but my ability to feel real passion is not there anymore. I love my husband–I really do. And when we do have sex, I enjoy it. But for me, it's just not a big priority anymore like it used to be."

The scenarios seemed to have the same common thread of apathy running through them. The women weren't totally turned off to sex, but it was certainly not a "big deal" to them anymore. Many complained that they didn't feel "sexy," were "too tired" at night or were "preoccupied" with daily problems. They no longer felt "sexually connected" enough with their husbands to want sex every night. However, there were a few women who said that it was their HUSBANDS who had the low sex drive. And although they would like to have sex more regularly, it wasn't "worth the hassle" of arguing with their husbands about it.

♥♥♥"WHEN I THINK BACK UPON THOSE FIRST FEW YEARS AND HOW NUTS WE WERE FOR EACH OTHER, IT MAKES ME SMILE. I LUSTED FOR HIM ALL THE TIME. FOREPLAY WAS NEVER LESS THAN AN HOUR AND I JUST MELTED TO HIS TOUCH. AFTER TEN YEARS OF MARRIAGE, IT'S STILL WARM AND LOVELY BUT DEFINITELY LACKS THAT FIRE AND SPARK IT HAD. I FEEL COMFORTABLE BUT IT ALL SEEMS SO ROUTINE. I GUESS WE JUST KNOW EACH OTHER TOO WELL."

♥**Level Of Passion During Intercourse**–Most of the women echoed the same sentiment. Sex had become fairly perfunctory and lacked the passion and spontaneity of previous years. Foreplay was drastically reduced in terms of time and the lengths they went to to please each other. In general, most of the women stated that their sex had become very "predictable." Although it wasn't totally unsatisfactory, they missed the "fireworks" of the old days. Most said that the foreplay consisted of some limited kissing and stroking but was mainly the act of intercourse, itself. About half of the women said that they reached orgasm only 50% of the time or less. This was because their husbands either weren't willing to take the time required for them to reach orgasm or they still weren't aware of how to successfully bring their wives to orgasm.

Most women were in agreement that it is unrealistic to expect the heat of passion to remain intense over many years. The common complaint was that the husbands "lacked imagination" and the "patience" necessary to create an aura of tenderness. They were also lacking in communication and seldom spoke loving words during lovemaking anymore. The bonding they had once established as a result of lengthy foreplay was gone. They said their husbands usually wanted to head "straight for their breasts and genitals" for a "little stroking" and then have intercourse right away. This was contributing to their lack of desire in many cases.

This woman's sentiments were echoed by many others who wrote to me: "When my husband and I get in bed and he immediately starts groping for my breasts without any loving words, it turns me off. It's almost like an invasion or a violation of my body. I know he loves me and I shouldn't be feeling this way, but I do. Without the 'flowers and candy' so to speak, sex feels like a purely physical act devoid of any loving intent. It's almost like I want to get it over with quickly, because there's nothing in it emotionally for me anymore."

It's interesting to note that over half of the women expressed a similar sentiment. It certainly strengthened the idea that *women deeply feel the need to be romanced.* And as the years go on, most women get less and less of this as part of their total sexual experience. As one woman put it, "I know I'm not going to get anything like I read about in romance novels. I don't expect that. But I do want to be held, petted and told how much I am loved. I know that if my husband did this for me then I would respond a lot better sexually to him. It's almost impossible for me to engage in sex for sex itself. It feels too empty. I hate feeling that he's only there to get off by using me and then it's over."

♥♥♥"SOMETIMES I WONDER IF ALL THE SEXUAL STUFF I DID WITH HIM BEFORE WE WERE MARRIED WAS JUST A KIND OF AUDITION. I WANTED TO PLEASE HIM AND MAKE HIM THINK I WAS

REALLY HOT STUFF. DON'T GET ME WRONG THOUGH, IT'S NOT LIKE I'M TURNED OFF TO SEX NOW. BUT I DON'T FEEL THE SAME ABOUT ORAL SEX AND SOME OF THE MORE WILD AND CRAZY STUFF I DID BEFORE. NOW IT MAKES ME FEEL KIND OF CHEAP. I KNOW IT SOUNDS CRAZY BUT I CAN'T HELP FEELING THIS WAY. I'D LOVE TO KNOW WHY."

♥**Techniques Used During Foreplay and Intercourse**–It was of special interest to me that so much of the sexual repertoire and techniques women used when dating or first married changed or were dropped later on in their marriages. Many of the women said they performed oral sex on their partners much more frequently before marriage. Many said that their attitudes toward it had changed from "losing interest," to feeling "uncomfortable" doing it, to downright "distasteful." They also stated that many of their husbands who regularly used to satisfy them with oral sex had also slacked off in their use of this technique. A few of them said they had even tried anal intercourse before marriage because the men really wanted them to do it. However, most of them found it to be "unacceptable" and said they wouldn't try it again. Some of the women also said that in their more "adventurous days" they used "mirrors, vibrators, porno films and other aids" to keep variety and spice in their sex lives. But now they felt "ridiculous" about employing these in their lovemaking. The women all echoed the same sentiment in one way or another. And it was that they felt like a "different person" now about their sexual views.

All of them agreed that the length and quality of their present foreplay was sharply reduced in comparison to the early days of their marriages. Where they used to spend approximately one half to an hour engaged in stroking, all over body kissing, massaging and the like, they seldom did any of that now.

One woman felt embarrassed about her previous sexual experiences: "When I look back at how we used to have phone sex and use vibrators and other love toys, I feel like blushing. I must have really enjoyed it back then, but for some reason I would feel uncomfortable doing those things now. I don't know whether it's because I'm a mother now and see myself differently or whether it was just a phase I outgrew."

♥♥♥"EVEN AFTER MY HUSBAND AND I HAD BEEN MARRIED FOR FIVE YEARS, WE USED TO SIT ON THE COUCH AND MAKE OUT LIKE TEENAGERS FOR AN HOUR. THE KISSING WAS SO WONDERFUL. IT DIDN'T ALWAYS LEAD TO INTERCOURSE, EITHER.

WE JUST LOVED THE FEELING OF OUR LIPS AND BREATH ON EACH OTHER. GOSH, IT WAS NICE! I DON'T KNOW WHY WE STOPPED DOING IT. I GUESS IT WAS AFTER THE KIDS CAME AND IT DIDN'T FIT INTO OUR SCHEDULES ANYMORE. BUT I REALLY MISS IT."

♥**Amount Of Kissing**–Almost all of the women said that after a few years of marriage, they seldom kissed their husbands passionately unless they were planning on having intercourse. Their kissing became limited to the usual "hello-goodbye" pecks on the cheek or quick lip kisses when their husbands left for work and came home at night. Most women said they still had some limited kissing during foreplay, but the practice of passionately exploring each other with their tongues and lips for hours was over.

A woman in her mid-thirties had this to say: "When I stop to think about it, the kissing during foreplay was highly arousing. I don't think I ever enjoyed anything as much as just making out. There was no pressure to perform. We did it just to delight in the wonderful warmth kissing brings to the body. Don't ask me why we don't do it as much as we used to. I guess we just got out of the habit somewhere along the line."

♥♥♥"WHEN I WATCH YOUNG COUPLES HOLDING HANDS AND KISSING IN PUBLIC I CAN'T HELP BUT FEEL SAD BECAUSE IT REMINDS ME OF HOW MY HUSBAND AND I ACTED WHEN WE FIRST STARTED GOING TOGETHER. IT MAKES ME FEEL OLD TO WATCH YOUNG PEOPLE DOING WHAT WE USED TO DO. WE WERE ALWAYS KISSING AND PROFESSING OUR LOVE TO EACH OTHER. BOY WERE WE MUSHY! BUT HOW TIMES HAVE CHANGED. IF I EVER GOT A LOVE NOTE FROM MY HUSBAND NOW, I'D PROBABLY THINK HE WAS FEELING GUILTY BECAUSE HE WAS HAVING AN AFFAIR!!"

♥**Display of Affection**–About 80% of the women said that after five years of marriage, they never held hands or kissed in public, or sent each other love notes or gifts for no reason. They admitted that the practice of all these little *courtship rituals* had died out over the years. Many of the women also felt inhibited about displaying too much affection in front of their children. They felt very uncomfortable about appearing *overtly sexual* in front of their kids. They felt it was not in good taste and it also embarrassed the kids.

One mother of three had this to say: "I get the feeling that our kids have a strong aversion to seeing anything too sexual going on between my husband and me. It's the old story that when kids think about their parents having sex it makes them nauseous! If my husband and I kiss a little too long in front of them, they kind of make themselves scarce or make some wisecrack. They don't hide the fact that it makes them feel uncomfortable. So over the course of time, I think it's contributed to my husband and I being a lot less demonstrative than we would be if they weren't around."

♥♥♥"IN THE BEGINNING OF OUR RELATIONSHIP WE WOULD NEVER RUN OUT OF THINGS TO TALK ABOUT. BUT AFTER 10 YEARS OF MARRIAGE IT SEEMS LIKE WE HAVE NOTHING LEFT TO TALK ABOUT. WHEN WE GO OUT TO DINNER ALONE, WE SIT IN SILENCE FOR HALF OF THE EVENING. IF WE AREN'T DISCUSSING THE KIDS, THERE ISN'T MUCH TO SAY TO EACH OTHER ANYMORE."

♥Level And Quality Of Communication–It is interesting to note that many women felt that the lack of passion in later years of marriage was directly attributable to a sharp decrease in communication with their spouses. They felt that in the early days when they talked a lot about themselves and their expectations from each other and their relationship, it served to keep them a lot closer emotionally. However, after years of the normal *wear and tear* on the relationships, many of them had built up insulating walls around themselves. This was due to a host of unresolved issues, some of which we will take up later. But the end result of the emotional walls was that it created a distance which had a profound negative affect on the level of passion between them. Many of the women made the same statement that although they deeply loved their husbands, they felt that the feeling of being in love with them was no longer there.

There were many women who voiced the same disappointment as this woman:

"After many years of marriage I really regret not having that feeling of being 'in love' with my husband. I love him, but the closeness between us which once existed is no longer there. I'm not sure why– but deep down I feel that the years of fighting, hurt feelings and disappointments have simply eroded that electric feeling of being in love. I guess I should dwell on the positive more often, but I can't help getting bogged down by all the negatives that have happened between us. We've put walls up around ourselves and the ability to touch each other's hearts seems no longer possible."

♥♥♥"AS WE GET OLDER, I WONDER DO WE ALL LOSE THE ABILITY TO REALLY HAVE FUN AND ENJOY THINGS TOGETHER LIKE WE USED TO? I CAN'T REMEMBER THE LAST TIME MY HUSBAND AND I REALLY HAD A HUGE LAUGH TOGETHER OR DID SOMETHING TOTALLY CRAZY THAT MADE US DELIRIOUSLY HAPPY."

♥**Fun And Enjoyment Experienced As A Couple**–The most prevalent consensus of feeling amongst the women interviewed was that after several years of marriage there was no longer enough time for them to enjoy the fun kinds of things they used to at the start of the relationship. There were too many commitments in terms of obligations to their jobs, their kids' needs and schedules, plus keeping their homes running smoothly. It left them with no spare time to enjoy doing things with their husbands. The couples who had been married for three years or more usually got to the movies once or twice a month and had dinner out alone at a restaurant less than once a month. A married woman of 10 years expressed her feelings this way: "If somebody gave me one wish that would come true, I'd wish for a month's vacation in Hawaii with my husband. I think we could learn to laugh together again, we would make love every day and recoup those old feelings of being totally in love. I wonder if it will ever happen again for us? The way our lives are so programmed with kids and working so hard, it will probably be another 10 years before we will ever get to do something like that. I feel so weighed down by our responsibilities, that I've become almost like a machine who isn't capable of laughter or enjoying anything anymore. I'm always too worried about the kids, money, health and everything else to really ENJOY my life. I detest this feeling but I have no idea how to change things to make it better."

This woman's sentiments echoed many others. I got the message loud and clear that the daily responsibilities of family and job were simply squeezing all the enjoyment out of them. And it's very true for all of us. When we were kids, we'd laugh at anything and enjoyed just about everything. But as we get older, it becomes increasingly difficult to strike a balance between work and play. *It feels like the cards are so stacked against us that we'll never be able to really play again with our mates like we did in the carefree days.*

♥♥♥"I WISH I HAD THE GUTS TO DISCUSS THIS WITH SOMEONE BUT I HAVEN'T–FOR MANY REASONS. WHAT I'D LOVE TO KNOW IS IF MOST WOMEN HAVE LOST THEIR SEX DRIVE AFTER YEARS OF MARRIAGE LIKE I HAVE. IT'S NOT LIKE I HATE DOING IT OR ANYTHING LIKE THAT, BUT I REALLY DON'T FEEL THE

SAME WAY ABOUT IT AS I USED TO. AT ONE TIME, I COULDN'T WAIT TO JUMP IN BED WITH MY HUSBAND AND MAKE LOVE FOR HOURS. BUT I JUST DON'T FEEL THAT KIND OF BURNING DESIRE ANYMORE AND HAVE NO IDEA HOW TO GET IT BACK OR EVEN IF IT'S POSSIBLE."

♥**Lack of Sexual Desire For Your Mate**–Similar statements were made by well over half of the women who wrote to me. It all boiled down to the feeling that after several years of marriage, they had lost the deep level of sexual desire for their husbands they had as newlyweds. They said that in the beginning of their relationships they really "wanted" to have sex frequently with their partners. They were often the "aggressors" in the relationship and felt they "couldn't get enough of the guy." But now they were a bit mystified as to why the feeling wasn't there anymore. It wasn't because they didn't *like* sex anymore; it was just that they didn't have the same *enthusiasm*. Many said they have to be "coaxed" by their husbands into having sex. However when they did, most said it was "pleasant" and they had forgotten how "good" it made them feel. But in the days afterwards, they just kind of *forgot* about that aspect of it and their old attitudes prevailed of *being too tired* or *not being in the mood*.

A woman who has been married for fifteen years wrote to me and summed it up by saying: "My husband kids me all the time by saying that 'he has to make an appointment with me to have sex.' He says it jokingly, but I know he has a certain amount of anger about it because it's true. God knows I love him, but in all honesty, I just can't seem to muster up those sexy kinds of feelings I used to have about him. This really bothers me. I often wonder if I'm the only one with this problem or do other women who have been married for a number of years feel the same way?"

In response to her question, I would tell this woman that there is good news and bad news. The good news is that, yes, she is not all alone in her feelings. An overwhelming number of women whom I interviewed feel exactly like she does. The bad news is that this should NOT be a normal occurrence in any marriage. *The desire for passion and great sex with your husband after many years of marriage should be and is possible for all women*. And in some later chapters we'll be discussing remedial techniques for putting the old zip back into your libidos.

♥♥♥"HOW CAN I FIND THE TIME TO HAVE A ROMANTIC RELATIONSHIP WITH MY HUSBAND? AFTER A DAY OF TENDING TO THREE KIDS, SOLVING EVERYONE'S PROBLEMS AND CLEANING

A 4 BEDROOM HOUSE, ROMANCE IS THE ONE THING I HAVE NO TIME OR ENERGY LEFT FOR."

♥**Difficulty Establishing The "Right" Atmosphere**–At least half of the women who complained about the lack of sexual passion in their marriages, admitted THEY were the ones having trouble "getting in the right mood" for sex. They said that the *timing* was always wrong and they were usually too "tired, stressed out or upset with their spouses" to feel the least bit *romantic*. Many said that after a grueling day tending to their kids, they simply lacked the energy it took to work themselves into a passionate state. Also, the *newness and excitement* of their younger days was gone and they found that their husbands didn't inspire the excitement or passion in them as they once did. It was not quite the case of "familiarity breeds contempt" but the lesser syndrome of "familiarity breeds boredom."

♥♥♥"SOMETIMES I FEEL LIKE NATURE CONSPIRES AGAINST ALL WOMEN TO PREVENT US FROM MAINTAINING A GOOD SEX LIFE. SINCE I'VE BEEN ABOUT 38 YEARS OLD, I'VE BEEN STRUGGLING WITH A LOW LIBIDO BECAUSE OF MENSTRUAL PROBLEMS AND OTHER HORMONAL DIFFICULTIES WHICH INTERFERE WITH MY SEXUAL ENJOYMENT. I FEEL LIKE I JUST CAN'T GET A BREAK IN THIS DEPARTMENT."

♥**Physical Changes**–Depending on their ages, many of the women reported that changes in their physical bodies was interfering with their levels of passion. Among the most commonly cited complaints were frequent PMS, vaginal dryness, menstrual problems, post-partum depression and various hormonal changes. They felt many of these problems which were more frequently found in women over 30 were preventing them from enjoying the act of intercourse, thus decreasing their sexual appetites and contributing to their overall lack of passion. Another very common issue was how their weight gain over the years negatively affected their self-esteem and how they perceived themselves in sexual terms. Many felt they looked stupid having sex when they were overweight and it made them increasingly self-conscious and inhibited about having intercourse. They shared a lack of desire to be seen naked by their husbands because they felt their bodies didn't live up to what they once were. Even though the husbands were reassuring that it didn't matter to them, the women usually felt strongly that their discontentment with their own bodies was responsible, in part, for depressing their sexual desires.

The most memorable of these collective sentiments was expressed by one woman in this sad disclosure: "I hate my body. I'm fat and flabby and I feel ashamed to have my husband see me naked. I always get undressed out of his sight because I think I must be a real turn-off to look at. My obesity makes me feel foolish when we're having sex. I keep picturing myself as a big fat cow trying to look and act sexy. I would be a lot more comfortable omitting sex entirely, until I can once again feel good about the way I look."

This particular problem is also a self-perpetuating one. The negative feelings brought on by being overweight lead to depression and made them eat more in an attempt to dull these painful feelings. We all know that food tends to bring a certain level of comfort to those suffering emotional pain. Therefore, the women affected found that it was terribly difficult to break the cycle and lose weight. Other women who were going through hormonal changes related to pregnancy, post-partum changes and menopause blamed a hormonal imbalance for their weight problems. They felt like they were fighting a battle in which they had little or no control. This led to further feelings of helplessness and depression. Some admitted that they had completely given up and accepted the fact that they would never be *svelte and sexy* again.

♥♥♥"IF YOU ASKED ME TO POINT OUT THE SINGLE BIGGEST FACTOR WHICH HAS KEPT MY HUSBAND AND I FROM ENJOYING ROMANTIC TIME TOGETHER I WOULD HAVE TO SAY IT'S OUR KIDS. WHEN YOU'RE KNEE-DEEP IN KIDS 16 HOURS A DAY, SEVEN DAYS A WEEK, HOW CAN ANYONE FIND TIME FOR ROMANCE WITH THEIR HUSBANDS? I CAN BARELY FIND TIME TO GO TO THE BATHROOM BY MYSELF, MUCH LESS FIND THE TIME FOR ROMANTIC DINNERS AND MAKING LOVE WITH MY HUSBAND. THERE WAS A TIME, BEFORE THE KIDS, WHEN WE DOTED ON EACH OTHER EVERY SECOND OF THE DAY. BUT REALISTICALLY, THAT'S NEVER GOING TO HAPPEN AGAIN. THE SENSE OF RESPONSIBILITY IN TRYING TO RAISE THREE KIDS IS COMPLETELY OVERWHELMING AND TIME CONSUMING. I GUESS WE'LL JUST HAVE TO PUT ALL THE HEARTS AND FLOWERS ON HOLD UNTIL THE KIDS ARE GROWN UP ENOUGH TO TAKE CARE OF THEMSELVES."

♥The Kids–Children were cited as the biggest obstacle of all in trying to keep that sense of romance and passion alive in most marriages. The paradox is that we were raised to believe that having kids would make our marriages stronger and cement the emotional bonds with our husbands by giving real purpose to our unions. However the reality is that kids monopolize our time, our emotions and become the focus of our existence especially when they're young. How many times have you heard women echo these sentiments: "Sure I'd love to spend more romantic time with my husband but where's it going to come from? My days are completely filled with raising our kids." Others said: "If we didn't talk about our kids, we'd probably have nothing to say to each other."

There is no doubt that raising kids is a full time proposition for couples. Most women adopt the attitude that it is totally impossible to maintain the same kind of active sex life that they had before the kids came. They feel that the best they can do is to strike some kind of balance between the two. However, there are women who BELIEVE AND PRACTICE the opposite. It is their actions and beliefs that we will explore later in our search for answers to these seemingly unsolvable situations.

CHAPTER 3

HOW DID IT HAPPEN??

ADDRESSING THE ISSUES

The rest of this book is going to be devoted to exploring the central issues raised in the first two chapters. We have heard from women about the factors that went into building passion, creating intimacy, and nurturing their relationships when they first began. The second chapter detailed what many women felt was lacking in their relationships after several years of marriage. In this chapter we are going to find out what created that BIG SPACE in–between and answer some pertinent questions about this void. Even though most of these marriages were not on the brink of divorce, the women were unhappy with their present situations. They all expressed the desire to recapture the feelings of passion and intimacy that seem to have been lost or overshadowed along the way.

AND THIS IS POSSIBLE. There are plenty of relationships that are successful and even more passionate than they were in their beginnings. Hopefully, what women in these types of relationships have to say and offer in the way of suggestions will provide some insights and revelations to others who would like the same. One thing is very important to bear in mind. It is not INEVITABLE that all long-term relationships will lose their passion. Too many women adopt the mind-set that this is "just how it is" and there is no possible way to avoid it. We are going to dispel this myth. And we must begin by recognizing that it is just this kind of thinking that will automatically set the relationship up for a fall. Marriages DO NOT have to breed boredom or dullness. On the contrary, it is every person's right and responsibility to keep their passion alive and growing in a marriage. We need to work as hard on this as we do in raising our children. We wouldn't even consider short-changing our kids of the love and devotion they deserve. We always find or make the time and energy it takes to nurture them. But we have to do the same for our spouses. And this is something we should do willingly for each other. *There is ALWAYS TIME if we are willing to create it.*

Summarizing the issues most prevalent in the first two chapters, the following topics are what we'll be concentrating on in the rest of the book:

1. Communication and Resentment
2. Nurturing and Priorities
3. Fun and Playtime
4. Kids
5. Intimacy
6. Arguments

And besides figuring out WHAT HAPPENED, we are going to devote time to REMEDIAL METHODS of making things right.

THE MEN SPEAK

Since every relationship is made up of two people, I think it's necessary to hear some of the male points of view about these issues. Sometimes we get so involved and overwhelmed with our own problems, we stop LISTENING to what our spouses have to say. Other times, we simply dismiss their point of view as being *ridiculous* and having *no validity*. This is a big mistake. I can't emphasize this point enough. No matter how far off base you feel his thinking might be, he is, after all, the other half of your relationship. And in order to solve the problems coming between you, you'll have to start placing some validity on what he's saying. You will have to do this in order to form any type of a compromise which can bring about a lasting resolution to the problem.

I asked women what their husbands had to say about the various issues we discussed. I wanted to see where the men were coming from emotionally and intellectually to get a more balanced picture on the subjects. I also asked them what THEY thought was happening in their marriages and relationships. This is what the men had to say:

SEX AND PASSION

♥"She never takes the role of aggressor in lovemaking anymore. If I didn't initiate sex, we'd never have it."

♥"My wife is so involved with the kids that I am literally squeezed out of the picture sexually. All I get is excuses about why she doesn't want to have sex. She's either too tired, has a headache, is too upset about something or has her period. Sometimes I feel like just giving up. I mean, I don't want to have to beg for sex, but it seems like this is what our sex lives have been reduced to."

♥"Nine times out of ten I get turned down when I reach over to touch her. She's always pissed off at me about something or other and is rarely in the mood."

♥"I'm always left with the feeling that my wife simply accommodates me for sex. She doesn't refuse me, but she shows very little enthusiasm about the whole thing. I don't feel wanted or desired anymore."

♥"Whenever I approach her for some sexual playing around, it's like I'm intruding on her space. She acts annoyed and says she is busy doing something or whatever excuse she can come up with to avoid me. She used to jump in bed with me at the drop of a hat. But now there is never a 'right time' to approach her."

REFUSAL AND REJECTION

As you can see, there are a lot of men who complain about the same thing–the lack of sexual responsiveness in their wives. From what they have stated, there is little doubt that plenty of women are showing a great deal of sexual apathy towards their husbands. And the fact is that many women openly ADMITTED to it in their statements from previous chapters. Many of them said they had lost a lot of their desire and sexual passion for their husbands but were at a loss to determine the exact causes. There were a few cases where it was the man who had lost his sexual appetite for his wife. But in 8 out of 10 cases, the lack of sexual response came from the WOMEN. Why this happens rarely has it's roots in just one cause. After years of marriage, there are any number of reasons why women turn off sexually to their mates. And in most cases it has nothing to do with the sex act itself. The roots lie mainly in two causes. One: the way women perceive themselves sexually—and Two: it is a direct result of an emotional and physical estrangement from their spouses which has built up over the years. We will discuss them both in-depth in a later chapter.

THE KIDS

♥"Don't get me wrong, I love my kids. But I think that my wife obsesses on them to the exclusion of everyone else in her life– especially me. We either have a baby between us in bed every night or she is totally absorbed in orchestrating all the kid's activities. It's impossible to get five minutes alone with her. I feel like her whole life is about the kids and I'm just an adjunct to it."

♥"My wife had our baby six months ago. But you would think by the way she acts, it was six hours ago. She's either too sore, having her period, nursing, or too bloated to have sex anymore. It's always some kind of hormonal excuse. I'm beginning to believe the men who say that there is no sex after kids."

♥"My wife and I are having a real problem because I don't want another child. We have two children and I feel that's enough. As it is, I'm pushed out of almost every facet of her life. If we had three, I might as well move to another home and just send her support checks."

♥"We spent 20 years battling over the kids. And now that they're grown and out of the house, I find that we have nothing left between us. I don't know what we could ever do to restore any closeness or good feelings between us at this stage of our lives."

♥"Nobody ever prepared me for the reality of what kids do to your sex life. After three kids in four years, my wife went from a 125 lb woman with a voracious sexual appetite to a 179 lb woman who is too frazzled to even think about sex much less do it."

ARE THE MEN JUSTIFIED IN THEIR FEELINGS?

I know what you women are thinking. The first thing is that these men probably don't ever help their wives with the kids and that's why the wives have no time for them. The second is that these men are all exaggerating their cases. But, wherever the problem lies, one thing is for sure. There are a lot of "unhappy campers" out there in terms of men who feel their kids are overshadowing their own emotional and sexual needs.

The question we all need to explore here is why this is happening in so many marriages. Are the women left with so many of the child rearing responsibilities that there is simply very little time left over to devote to their husbands? And if so, is this the fault of the husbands because they aren't contributing to their share of those responsibilities? Or is this just an unavoidable reality of what happens when you have kids? There's also the question of whether women actually do lose a lot of their sexual passion because they have to fulfill the role of being a full-time Mom. Do they begin to view themselves as less sexual because they can't reconcile the roles of 'Mom' and 'Lover?' Could the wives possibly resent their husbands because the parenting is left mainly up to them and therefore, their sexual appetites lessen out of ill–will and mis-communication?

In my opinion, the lack of communication which leads to built-up resentment between couples is the SINGLE MOST detrimental factor which squeezes the sex and romance out of marriages. We will take up the proposed questions and give some insights as well as answers to them in a later chapter. However, I will reiterate that this is one TOUGH problem. And assigning blame one way or the other will certainly not make it go away. It is a given that women are going to devote all of their energies to trying to raise happy, well–adjusted kids. However, our concern is whether it has to be done at the expense of our marital relationships. Most women enter marriages believing that children will act to strengthen their relationships. But when they are in the time-consuming situation of raising them, many of these same women begin to act and feel differently. Later, we'll hear from women who have successfully overcome this problem and how they did it.

FUN AND PLAYTIME

♥"The one thing I miss most with my wife is the fun we had together before we got married. I understand that marriage, kids and responsibilities limit the amount of activities and spontaneity we once had. But it seems like my wife has lost all her playfulness. She used to make jokes during sex and laugh hysterically during movies and do other silly things. Now, she's so serious. She says that all her responsibilities with the kids and housework leaves no time to have fun anymore. But I think that's just an excuse. She doesn't seem to enjoy ME anymore."

♥"I remember the days when my wife would make a fun event out of anything. She had great ideas about ways to spend time. Like on Sundays, she'd make a picnic for us during football games and we'd spread a blanket out on the floor and enjoy it. Nowadays she's too busy with the laundry or driving the kids someplace to sit with me for even 10 minutes and watch the game. I miss all the togetherness we had."

♥"There was a time when my wife couldn't get to a party fast enough. We always had a ball laughing it up with our friends and having a few drinks. Now that we're raising a family, I guess she thinks it means an end to the good times. She doesn't want to party anymore–and forget having a drink. It just isn't happening for us like it used to."

♥"My wife and I used to laugh about everything together. I don't know what happened but we don't do that anymore. I can't remember one time in the past few years when we've sat down and gotten silly about anything. Life has just gotten too serious."

♥"My wife doesn't go for sports anymore. When we were dating, we used to go to games, go skating, run and bicycle together. Whenever I ask her to do something fun now, she's always 'too busy.' I really love my wife but I can see why guys say that all the fun stops once you get married."

SO WHAT REALLY HAPPENED?

It's ironical when you hear both sides. The women say that the men don't want to DO ANYTHING except sit in front of the TV and watch football. The men say that the women just aren't FUN anymore. So where does the truth lie? From what these men are saying, it sounds like the wives are much too busy with raising their families to make time for real enjoyment with their husbands. Granted, the responsibilities of raising a family, keeping a home and working, does in reality, alter one's lifestyle. *Fun time doesn't just HAPPEN anymore without some planning.* There has to be planning for babysitters, re-arranging household schedules and a lot more when there's a family to consider rather than just two people. In a later chapter, some women will tell you how they have successfully managed to do it.

What I frequently hear from the husbands is that they think their wives have lost the ability to laugh and experience fun WITH THEM. They miss that one-on-one kind of fun. This sentiment is echoed by both sides. Does marriage have to mean the "end of the party?" Why aren't couples enjoying things together like they used to? *The answer is that the couples aren't enjoying EACH OTHER like they used to.* And once again, the main culprit is that *lack of communication* which is so vital in keeping couples bonded and intimate.

ARGUMENTS

♥"The problem with my wife and all women as far as I'm concerned is that they don't know how to argue fairly. My wife and I will be arguing about the kids and suddenly she's bringing up things I did to her ten years ago. And in my mind I'm thinking 'Wow, here we go again. Can't she ever forget anything that's in the past?' So we end up fighting even more about stupid things that have nothing to do with the kids. I feel like I just can't win."

♥"I am so sick of being nagged at and told everything I do is wrong that I just clam up when she starts in on me. I figure there's no way I can defend myself because the lady has an answer for EVERYTHING. It's easier to just keep my mouth shut and tune her out."

♥"What I really hate about the fights my wife and I have is how she gets so PERSONAL in her attacks. We always start out arguing about a specific THING and then it escalates to the point where she tells me what a lousy husband I am and how insensitive I am, etc. I'd rather walk away from her rather than stay there and be the brunt of all her insults."

♥"When my wife gets mad at me, it's never for just a few hours. No matter what we argue about, she goes on seething for days. I get the 'silent treatment' which I hate. I don't understand why she has to carry such resentment around with her. Her resentment makes it impossible for there to ever be any peace in the house."

♥"My wife's biggest problem is that she never LISTENS to my side when we're having a fight. She's too busy butting in with all her snide comments to actually hear what I have to say. She's too interested in planning her rebuttal to take the time to really listen to any of MY feelings on the subject."

WHY IT'S HAPPENING

We have always been told that arguing is a "healthy" thing in a relationship. Well, this happens to be true. Couples need to discuss their problems–not argue about them. We are two separate individuals with different opinions, feelings and points of view. And the secret of successfully overcoming these differences is to try to bring these feelings to the table and resolve them. Naturally, two individuals can't agree on everything. There are going to be times when we are able to agree with each other, times when we can reach a compromise and other times when we truly reach a "Mexican Standoff." This is normal. However, the problems come about not because of the fact that we ARE differing, it's the *WAY WE PROCESS*.

From what these men are saying, it is clear that they are involved in situations where the discussions have become destructive arguments instead of constructive resolutions. The red flags apparent in the comments from the men are as follows:

- Not listening to the other person
- Personal attacks on the other person
- Drawing unrelated or past problems into the present argument
- The deadly silent treatment
- Never resolving the argument to both parties satisfactions

Destructive arguing fosters long-term resentments on both sides which will eventually be a death knell for the marriage. If the couples are communicating resentment, misunderstanding and ill–will toward each other, there can never be true passion, enjoyment and nurturing in the relationship. We'll be talking about these destructive arguments in-depth in a later chapter especially devoted to this problem.

INTIMACY

♥"To me, intimacy means having a very special bond between a man and a woman in which the love between you transcends everything. It's knowing your partner to the core of their being. It's a no-holds barred kind of interaction in terms of loving and receiving love. In the beginning of our marriage, this is what my wife and I had. After 11 years, we have retained some of those feelings but have a lost a lot more than I bargained for over the years."

♥"My regrets lie with the loss of the sexual intimacy in our marriage. There was a time where we craved each other physically to the extent that it was the main focus of our lives. After being married for six years, our intimacy has changed dramatically. My wife no longer desires the same sexual menu we once had. I feel like she has built a wall around herself and has made certain acts 'off-limits' now. She makes me feel like certain intimate acts are an invasion of her now rather than desiring me as she once did."

♥"Is there still intimacy in our marriage? Yes and no. I mean my wife still likes sex and everything, but she's a lot more inhibited about little things. She avoids being naked in front of me or talking dirty during sex or just being openly sexual with me. I don't know if it's ME, or just that she's embarrassed about her body."

♥"My wife and I used to be extremely intimate with each other. We'd have sex during the afternoons and lust for each other so much that we couldn't wait to get home from a party and make love. We don't do this anymore. She's always finding some excuse to put sex off. It seems like this has become the rule rather than the exception."

♥"I would refer to intimacy as a couple's private time together–when they can get totally lost in each other and nothing else exists for the moment. Pretty poetic, huh? Well, we don't have it. I can't think of one minute in the day when a kid isn't crying, the phone isn't ringing or someone's not at the door selling something. Now you tell me–how does a couple go about finding intimacy in this circus-like environment?"

IS INTIMACY DIFFERENT FOR MEN AND WOMEN?

It's interesting to note that most of the men equated intimacy with sex. What's more, they felt that a couple needed to be alone to experience intimacy. However, when the women talk about intimacy, it's in terms of being close on an emotional and spiritual level as well as a sexual one. This raises the question as to whether men, in general, view the concept of intimacy the same way women do. From the statements they have made, it seems to mean two different things to each of the sexes.

But the one thing the mens' complaints had in common was that they felt their wives had turned down the flames of sexual intimacy a great deal over the course of their marriages. They are all saying, in one way or another, that their wives are not accepting them willingly on a sexual level as they once did. So how do we go about reconciling the problem when the sexes are coming from two different ideologies? The crux of the issue is that most men feel intimacy can only be experienced through sex, whereas women tend to take a far broader view. *Men and women have got to define what they mean as intimacy and communicate what they want from each other in terms of their own expectations.* This is crucial to finding any common ground or resolution to their dissatisfactions. The good news is that there are many couples who are successful in doing this. But it takes some very specific communication to reach that goal. We'll explore how other couples achieve this goal in a later chapter.

NURTURING AND PRIORITIES

♥"There are many women who don't understand how hard it is for a man to always be the strong one in a relationship. We not only have to be the breadwinners but also the emotional strength for the family. I think that women forget we are human beings too who have a need to express our own fears and sadness. But we are taught that men shouldn't do this for fear the women may think it shows weakness. I don't think that men get the nurturing they need or deserve in many marriages, mine included. Wives are too preoccupied giving all of it to the kids, but expect us to give it to them. So who's left to give it to us?"

♥"My marriage is for the most part very happy. But, if you asked me to pick out one thing that bothers me, it would be that I feel like I am no longer the number one priority in my wife's life. Sometimes I feel like I come last on her list. There's the kids, the housework, her clubs, her girlfriends and a lot of other things that take up her time. I don't get the special attention I used to like when we were dating. She used to give me backrubs, ask me about my work and shower me with a lot more sexual attention back then."

♥"I guess I'm at fault too, but it seems like we never have the time to give each other the emotional support we need. In the beginning of our relationship, we were never too busy to try to fix what was bothering the other. But now our lives have become so filled with obligations that I feel like I'm a ship drifting alone out there most days."

♥"My wife is always telling me that I never speak kindly to her anymore. Well you know what? She doesn't do it either. She's always finding fault or pointing out when I screw up. I don't think she ever stops to consider that kindness and consideration goes both ways."

THE BIG VOID

My, oh my. What I'm hearing loud and clear is that these men feel ABANDONED in their marriages. They have all stated that before the marriage, or in the beginning of the marriage, they felt like all their needs were being met by their partners. But with the responsibilities of marriage and family, they were the ones who got lost in the shuffle. This is something we need to take a careful look at in our own relationships. The man who said he gets tired of always being the strong one who gets no nurturing made a good point. I think a lot of women fall into this kind of erroneous thinking. This is not to diminish the emotional stretching women have to do. Granted, our kids need full-time support. We have other people we nurture too. However, could we be unintentionally neglecting our husbands? We might admit to it but quickly add that they neglect us too. Women feel that men have their work or sports or other things that take a priority in their lives.

The truth is that it's common for both sides to drop the ball in the nurturing department. *But assigning blame isn't the answer.* It doesn't restore what's lacking in the relationships. We need to identify the areas in which we are BOTH lacking and take responsibility for correcting it. When any person, male or female, feels neglected and unappreciated resentment is going to fester. The "why should I bother– he doesn't do it for me" attitude creeps in and sets us up for further neglect. And the vicious cycle keeps snowballing until the relationship is suffering more than the individuals who comprise it. There will be a chapter devoted to the topic of identifying and restoring the nurturing for both men and women in their relationships.

COMMUNICATION

♥"Boy, if there is ONE word I wish my wife never heard of it's 'communication.' All I hear about is how I'm not 'really communicating' with her! The whole thing is so stupid. I DO talk to her all the time. But she says I'm not really 'LISTENING.' She watches talk shows all day and gets her head filled with all this psycho-babble garbage. It's all us guys ever hear about nowadays– how we are 'insensitive' and don't 'communicate' properly. I think I speak for most guys when I say that we men deserve a break."

♥"I never thought I had a problem communicating with my wife but apparently she thinks differently. She's always telling me that I don't understand her needs because I don't HEAR what she's trying to say. This whole issue is very confusing to me. The truth is that I do take the time to listen to her. I can't understand why she's always saying I don't."

♥"My wife's idea of perfect communication is for me to keep my mouth shut while she complains about everything that's wrong in her life."

♥"I guess, unlike Reagan, I'm not much of a 'communicator.' I've always been kind of quiet. When I get home from work, I like to just sit in front of the TV or read the paper and try to wind down from the stresses of the day. But what I get instead is my wife immediately complaining about how hard her day was or how bad the kids were and that I must speak to them right away. What I wouldn't give for one hour of peace and quiet! Many times I'll just disappear into the bathroom to get a few minutes of solitude. My wife hates it when I do this. She doesn't understand that there are times when I do not want to communicate–I just want some peace and quiet. I don't think she has the right to blow it out of proportion by saying I don't know how to communicate with anybody."

♥"Do I think my wife and I communicate as well as we did when we first fell in love and got married? The answer is yes and no. Yes, I think we communicate very well about issues having to do with our kids, other people and events in our lives. But no, I feel we don't communicate on an intimate level about ourselves and our needs. I think we are both to blame. We spend all our time taking care of everyone else around us and don't leave enough time for taking care of each other."

WHAT THEY'RE COMPLAINING ABOUT

I think you'll agree that the same issues keep cropping up over and over again in the mens' dialogue. And the central theme is that there's not enough POSITIVE husband-wife communication going on in their relationships. In general, the men feel that the communication between them and their wives is mainly based on criticism of them without allowing for any self-defense. We're also hearing that same old complaint about their wives expending too much energy on everyone else around them, leaving little or no attention for the husbands. The husbands feel like all their efforts are going unnoticed and aren't being appreciated for their own contributions.

Establishing a positive dialogue between couples is the basis for every sound relationship. And dialogue shouldn't be reserved only to voice complaints. In recalling what the women said in a previous chapter, they feel that the men in their relationships become less communicative over time. So when they do get their husbands' "ears," the first thing that pours out of the wives is a litany of their dissatisfactions. The men, in turn, shut down because it adds too much stress to their already stressful day. This sets up a cycle where each side tunes the other out, attempting to get their complaints heard first. However, this cycle is doomed for failure because it's impossible to reach a resolution when both parties feel the other has ignored their needs. Each side becomes aware of the futility in the situation and a pattern of communicative avoidance gets established. Communication is the one theme that underlies all the other issues. And when healthy communication breaks down in a relationship, all the other facets from sex to patience to nurturing inevitably break down too.

The next chapter will examine many forms of negative communication during arguments. There will be helpful suggestions given on how to avoid the most common pitfalls that lead to destructive communication.

CHAPTER 4

HOW ARGUMENTS KILL PASSION

COUNTERPRODUCTIVE ARGUMENTS:
THE BOA CONSTRICTOR

From my research and the letters I have received, one thing has become very clear to me. There is NO SINGLE factor which suddenly appears after a year or two of marriage that begins to extinguish the flames of passion and intimacy between a man and woman. Instead, it's a combination of factors which slowly SQUEEZE the sparks and the passion out of a relationship.

This chapter is about the kinds of destructive and unresolved arguments which occur between couples. And I believe that these should be at the head of the list when enumerating problems in terms of their destructive powers to a relationship. I think *we would all agree that communication is EVERYTHING in a relationship.* It's the mesh that keeps couples bonded and in-tune with each other. We often hear young couples in love refer to themselves as "soulmates." What this means to me is that their art of inter–communication is so strong that it has allowed each of the partners to understand the other, *inside and out.* The term *soulmates* may sound mystical but it isn't. In reality, it simply means that one knows the other's wants, desires, needs, hopes, likes and dislikes so well, they are on a perfect wavelength–completely in tune with each other. And they got to that place by communicating OFTEN, HONESTLY AND POSITIVELY with each other. Each partner's awareness of the other's needs is so keen that one can anticipate them in many instances before they are voiced.

I believe that what unfortunately begins to happen over the course of many marriages is:

1: The communication between the partners decreases proportionately as other family member's needs and various factors place increasingly more pressure on each individual's time.

2: The NATURE of the communication between the partners changes. It starts out on a constructive level then slowly deteriorates to a point where it is very negative and counter–productive, thus, discouraging further communication.

COMMUNICATION AND ARGUMENTS

We have all heard countless times that arguing can be a good thing in a marriage. We are told that arguments mean we are communicating by getting out our grievances and feelings, and we should do this to keep our marriages healthy. To a degree, this is true. However, the danger occurs when the arguments become too frequent, too vitriolic and aren't resolved to either party's satisfaction. This will discourage any further communication and eventually the spouses will become resentful of each other. And I firmly believe that *it is the RESENTMENT which builds up over time between couples who argue and NEVER RESOLVE their differences that eventually squeezes every bit of love and passion out of a marriage.* And as this happens, INDIFFERENCE takes their place. Many people eventually get into a pattern of reacting with SILENCE because of the other person's intractability. Yet it is this silence borne out of resentment which is going to eventually erode the foundation of the marriage. *When the art of good communication stops so will the sex, the passion, the fun and the love.* Resentment seethes and boils within the individuals, making any healing between them really difficult.

And women, especially, find that it's nearly impossible to have good sex or generate any passion with a man who they resent and are always angry at. Women need tenderness, gentleness and a feeling that *everything is right* in the relationship in order to relax and express themselves passionately during sex. And when there's an ongoing undercurrent of resentment present, she's NEVER going to be in the mood. The husbands, in turn, don't really understand the basis of her feelings and usually interpret it as a rejection of them and their sexuality. She may not even be aware that this is causing her to feel "turned off" to making love with him. But it's one of the major reasons why sex dies a slow death in long-term relationships. And when the sex goes, eventually so does everything else. So it's vitally important to really understand the idea of how negative communication will suffocate marriages over time if it isn't addressed and corrected.

In the course of any relationship, especially a marriage, there are going to be thousands of situations in which a strong difference of opinion will lead to an argument. This is healthy and normal. We all have different perspectives which need to be heard and understood by the other party. Both may not necessarily agree with each other but they must be aired. One party may try to sway the other into thinking as they do. This may happen in some instances, but for the most part the other person will not change their opinion on a subject. When this happens, it's crucial that the couples learn to COMPROMISE and reach a workable solution they can both live with. *It may not be exactly what each had aimed for in the beginning, but both parties must remember that the RELATIONSHIP is ultimately MORE IMPORTANT than what the individuals in it want for themselves.* Compromise must be seen as a technique where the RELATIONSHIP GAINS rather than each person having to GIVE SOMETHING UP." More about this later.

HOW TO STRENGTHEN COMMUNICATION SKILLS

So how do we go about arguing constructively and avoiding the pitfalls which lead to the erosion of marriage over time? Well, I believe that the very first step in conquering any problem is to become aware of exactly WHAT WE ARE DOING WRONG. And only AFTER we have identified and become aware of how destructive our interaction is can we begin to change it. I am going to outline some of the most common pitfalls in the ways we argue and try to identify what category or categories people fall into.

* * * THE NAGGERS * * *

How many times have we heard from men that all their wives do is nag at them? And the wives' pat answer is: "If he listened to me and did what I asked of him, I wouldn't HAVE TO NAG him all the time."

There is truth on both sides in this common situation. Women do keep nagging because the men turn A DEAF EAR to them. This cycle brings about nothing but discouragement. Nobody listens and nothing gets resolved. So women keep asking themselves "HOW DO I GET HIM TO LISTEN TO ME THE FIRST TIME?" Well, the good news is that it's possible, but it's going to take some time and patience to break this cycle. When nagging and complaining become SO PERVASIVE that the other party becomes de-sensitized to it, they just *shut down*. They *tune you out* in an effort to shield themselves from further *attacks* which they take as a very personal assault. And at the stage when *complete shutdown* occurs, it's going to rapidly eat away at your marital relationship. When one party believes that the other isn't EVEN LISTENING to them, much less doing what they're being asked, the stage is set for our old enemy RESENTMENT. The men feel they are getting no respect from their wives and the wives feel they are being totally ignored.

Even though both may be true, who's right and who's wrong isn't the issue here any longer. It's gone way beyond that point and needs immediate correction.

HOW TO REPAIR IT

The first thing to recognize about any marriage or long-term relationship is this: Over the years there will be a million valid things you could complain about. But you certainly can see the negative impact it will have on your relationship if you continually do this. So–PICK YOUR SPOTS CAREFULLY. Situations and events have to be weighed in the entire SCHEME OF THINGS. It's most important that you sift through the maze of your anger and decide what's REALLY upsetting you. Then communicate your disapproval on the issues that really merit attention or on those matters in which you can truly effect a positive change. You'll need to make a lot of concessions about the smaller things that may be just as easy to solve or do yourself. So keep silent on those and just move on!

Now there are those who would argue that this isn't fair to women. You might think, "why should we have to do things ourselves that he should be doing too?" On the one hand, yes, you may be right. But on the other, *you have to keep the BIG PICTURE in mind* when you are striving to maintain a happy and healthy relationship. Nagging about every single thing that displeases you is going to cause a shutdown of your spouse and wreck your relationship over the course of five, ten or twenty years. You have to begin looking at it in terms of what's more important–your being right about every issue or just allowing some issues to dissolve on their own in order to keep your marriage from becoming a battlefield. And I know you'll agree that it's a lot wiser and less emotionally wrenching to learn to become selective about which problems you'll choose to vocalize. This does not mean you have to stuff your feelings!

BACKING OFF

When the relationship has reached the stage of silent, smoldering resentment, you're both overdue for a big TIME-OUT so you can get it back on track. You'll need to back off for several days until your spouse has begun to relax and begin the process of de-sensitization. Then it's a time to THINK POSITIVELY and try to keep all your future conversations with him on that level. In time, this will bring him back to a place where he's going to be more open to LISTENING to you again. And once he's not enveloped in his lead wall of isolation anymore, you can begin to change the way in which you interact.

When you have a "bone to pick" or some major complaint which needs resolution, remember, it has to be done in an environment free from hostility. Keep the nagging tone out of your voice because the tone itself will make him shut down all over again. The complaint has got to be discussed in a conversational way using the approach that "we have a problem" and "we both need to make some adjustments" to solve it. *Lecturing, condescension and nagging are NEVER GOING TO WORK.* They never did and they absolutely won't now. It's important to treat each other like adults–not like you're scolding a guilty child. A condescending manner will only get the door slammed in your face. Remember that every man and woman has the right to be treated with dignity and respect. *Your approach* is crucial in getting your point across.

This scenario illustrates how to go about getting results in a positive way:

THE OLD YOU: "This is the fifth Saturday in a row that I've asked you to finish cleaning out that pig-sty of a garage! Every week you promise you'll do it and what happens? Nothing–that's what. I am so sick and tired of having to yell at you to get you to move your butt and do this one thing. The only way that garage will ever get cleaned out is if I do it myself!"

THE NEW YOU: " Guess what, honey? I've decided to set the weekend aside and help you finish cleaning out the garage. We need to clear all the old junk out and make room to store our patio furniture for the winter. We can work until noon and then take a break for lunch. With the two of us working together, I think we can finish the job by tomorrow. Will you please help me?"

* * * *BEING CRITICAL* * * *

The next level in the escalation of negative communication is when you begin using criticism and attacking the character of a person rather than a specific behavior. In other words, it's when you bring the entire argument down to a personal level which is far more damaging to the relationship than carping or complaining about things. Personal attacks can be accurately described as "going straight for the jugular."

This type of negative communication is used for a variety of reasons. Some people just naturally fight this way because they have seen it done in their own families. But more often it's a kind of retaliation which is borne out of long term frustration. For example, if a woman is constantly complaining to her husband that he doesn't help her by picking up his own clothes and this is met with inaction and a deaf ear year after year, her frustration level intensifies. She feels that if she attacks on a stronger level, it will produce the desired results. This is when the argument goes FROM:

"Honey, how many times do I have to tell you to pick up your clothes? I have enough to do around here without following you around and cleaning up your messes."

TO:

"I don't know how you became such a pig. You are such a slob. Did you grow up in a pig sty?"

In comparing the two statements, it's apparent that the difference lies in the approach. The latter is aimed to bring him down a peg and make him feel like the inferior person she perceives him to be. It's used as a tool to psychologically abuse the other person. Furthermore, the huge pitfall here is that the other person has no other recourse than to react with total defensiveness. He will spend all his energies trying to defend himself and the real issues are completely lost in the process. He lashes back with anger to defend himself and she continues to sail on the same course of criticism. And neither will take the right steps toward setting things right.

These are the kinds of fights that invariably dissolve into a situation where neither party LISTENS to the other. Rather, they each keep repeating their own positions and nothing ever gets resolved. And as I have stated before, when you have no resolution then RESENTMENT just oozes out onto every facet of your lives. People who are stuck in resentment give up on communicating, their bonding and closeness goes out the window and their sex-lives suffer as a direct result.

THE REMEDY

As with any other destructive behavior, you must first become aware of what you are doing. You'll need to begin listening to yourself carefully every time you enter into an argument or even when you are making statements to the other person. You have to be very, very honest with yourself. Review what you have said. And then ask yourself these questions:

1. Was this a nasty personal attack meant to hurt his self–esteem?

2. Could I have gotten my point across in a much more positive way?

3. Did I criticize him as a person rather than simply stating what was bothering me about his behavior?

4. Did I speak in a sarcastic tone of voice?

5. Was my approach reasonable?

If you find that this has become the rule rather than the exception in the way you communicate with your spouse, it's got to be changed right away. The fastest way of alienating your spouse is by insinuating that you don't like who he is as a person. It's the same as telling him you have no respect for him. And this is not just going for the jugular, it's killing the victim. What's more, it's killing the marriage.

You can state the problem about his refusal to pick up after himself without dragging his character into it in this way:

"Honey, I am really frustrated. I need your help with this problem. It would make my job so much easier if you would please hang your clothes up or put them in the laundry basket. Please help me with this because I hate to become a nag and ruin our day complaining. But I need your cooperation. Can you help me?"

There's an old adage that you can catch a lot more flies with honey than with vinegar. Here you are asking for his help and appealing to him on a non-combative, non-destructive level. Even if you have to repeat this plea for a few weeks, it's going to be hard for him to ignore you when you are being so darn NICE about it. It's important to remember that we have evolved past childhood and earned our adulthood. Nobody wants to be scolded like a child anymore. It only perpetuates bad feelings and gets negative results.

IF YOUR SPOUSE IS THE CULPRIT

If your spouse always attacks you personally, then the same goes for him. But it's up to YOU to make him aware of what he's doing. You'll need to remember portions of his conversation and cite examples of his destructive words. Discuss it calmly and leave the criticism out of it in order to make your point. He is going to be a lot more receptive to your explanations in a non-combative environment. Analyze the fight for him. Point out the hurtfulness of the personal attack. Then go on to explain how the adverse effects of personal attack go far beyond the initial argument. Tell him that his condemnation of you is making you so defensive that you want to distance yourself from him emotionally and physically. And this will eventually, if it hasn't already, include the bedroom. Tell him that his criticism is making an emotional gulf between you which is getting harder and harder to bridge.

Men have to be told how this built-up resentment will directly affect them. As hard as it may seem to understand, most men don't get this concept. They have to have it spelled out for them. So do it. Tell him that YOU:

1. DO NOT WANT TO MAKE LOVE TO A MAN WHO BELITTLES YOU.

2. DO NOT WANT TO MAKE LOVE TO A MAN WHO YOU ARE OFTEN ANGRY AT.

3. DO NOT WANT TO MAKE LOVE TO A MAN WHO YOU BEAR GREAT RESENTMENT AGAINST.

Believe me, there are a lot of men for whom this will come as a great revelation. They have never truly understood the fact that women need a nurturing, positive, esteem-building environment in order to function at their sexual best. No one will ever convince me that they have the best sex of their lives after a nasty argument. And if they think they do, it's because they have a sick kind of need to be punished. Love flourishes in a loving environment. *Making love to a person you resent and have bitterness towards is a perversion of the act of love itself.*

SILENCE IS NOT GOLDEN

When destructive arguing gets so prevalent that one or both parties will not even attempt to communicate anymore, it brings about a situation that is almost impossible to repair. The marriage may go on, but it's going to be an empty shell. The feeling that there is NO FAIRNESS left in the other person will inevitably lead to the position of TOTAL ESTRANGEMENT. And at this point, the relationship, as you previously knew it, is over.

From what women have told me, I find that it is the man who is much more likely to retreat into a wall of silence than the woman. I believe this happens because of the way men and women are raised. Women are taught to express their feelings. They have the luxury of growing up in a support system of other women. They have their mothers and sisters and best girl-friends to confide in throughout much of their lives. Women are much more uninhibited about sharing their marital problems with other women and seeking their advice. I have said it before in my other books. Women act as psychiatrists to other women. They spend hours analyzing, comparing, and exploring feelings and problems. As a result, *women are much more IN TOUCH with their feelings.* Men do not grow up with this luxury. They are taught to internalize their feelings and in many cases to *avoid* them. And because they react this way, it takes them a lot longer to recover from an upset. Many times they avoid the conflict by PHYSICALLY REMOVING themselves, i.e. by walking out of the room. This leaves the female standing there seething in unresolved anger. And when he comes back into the room, she attacks with contemptuous words to try and draw him into the fight again. And all the while the man is internalizing to himself, "That bitch. I don't have to take her crap. I'm out of here." And he walks away again. And of course this kind of stonewalling solves absolutely nothing and further escalates the feelings of estrangement.

THE REMEDY

When you have reached this pit of negative interaction, it's going to take intensive and extensive work to repair the damage already done. Plus, it is going to take an equal amount of hard work to break this pattern of behavior. As we have said before, it is a behavior developed over a lifetime. But *EVEN THOUGH OLD HABITS DIE HARD, CHANGE IS NOT IMPOSSIBLE.*

I would recommend counseling for both parties when things have degenerated to this level. Emotional as well as behavioral changes have to be effected for both parties. There is an enormous amount of healing which has to take place because of the destruction done to the relationship and the deep resentment which it has caused. A competent marriage or relationship counselor should be able to guide the way and start some healthy restorative communication between you. *But first you BOTH have got to admit and fully understand the ramifications of this destructiveness which you have allowed into your marriage.* Once you have acknowledged and truly understood it, then and only then, will a counselor be able to help set things on a healing course. You also both have to agree that there is enough love left in your relationship to justify the hard course of remedial work ahead.

* * * THE INTERRUPTER * * *

A very common problem many men and women have with their communication is that they do not listen to the other person because they are always INTERRUPTING in order to make their own point. Interrupters often fabricate internal scripts in their heads and blurt them out before the other person has finished voicing his or her thoughts. The minute the interrupter hears something he doesn't agree with, he cuts in attempting to invalidate what the other is saying. It's not hard to predict that the recipient of the interruptions will shut down over time and become either non–responsive or non-participatory. No one wants to feel like they are in a "one-way battle" in which their opinions will never be heard much less considered.

The following is a scenario of the interrupter and how he operates:

HE: "I am firmly against our daughter getting her own car because she lacks the necessary maturity to have one. Let me explain why..."

(Once she hears the key words "lacks maturity" she doesn't hear another word he says. She is busy formulating her own response to that thought and breaks in before he has finished his thought.)

SHE: "Not mature enough? What the hell are you talking about? You let Billy have a car when he was sixteen and he certainly didn't show the maturity Dawn has at seventeen. You're being sexist and unfair. You couldn't possibly give me ONE valid reason why she's immature."

HE: "Well, if you'd shut up and let me finish for once, I 'll give you plenty of reasons. For one..."

SHE: (Interrupting again.) "I know what you're going to say. You are going to drag up that one isolated incident when she had a fender bender last year. But you KNOW it wasn't her fault. It was clearly that old jerk's fault who ran into her in the parking lot."

HE: "I wasn't going to say that at all. If you'd just let me finish I'll tell you ..."

(Meanwhile, she's still not listening. She's thinking "Boy, here we go again. I don't know why he's so unfair with Dawn. It makes me sick how he favors Billy. He's just so damn unreasonable when it comes to her." At this point she interrupts again.)

SHE: "Yeah, I've heard it all before. Now I suppose I'm going to hear all about how she doesn't have a job and can't help with the car payments. You'll never cut her a break. I don't know why we are even discussing this because your mind is totally closed on the subject."

HE: "No it isn't. You're the one with the closed mind. Please. Just hear me out on this. You'll have to admit that Dawn has shown no responsibility about anything. For example, she still refuses to clean up her room..."

SHE: (interrupting again) "Her room? You're bringing up her room? What's that got to do with a car? How far-fetched are you going to go to build your stupid case against her?"

HE: "I give up. You won't even give me the courtesy of allowing me to finish one sentence..."

(He starts walking out of the room in complete frustration.) SHE: "Sure–walk away from me like you always do. You know you're wrong and have no real argument."

(She keeps shouting at him even when he disappears into the next room.)

In this scenario, whether he is wrong or right about his daughter is not the point. The point is that he has an opinion and she is not giving him an opportunity to express it. She is not respecting him enough as a person to really listen to what he's saying and consider it carefully. She is cutting him off at each and every turn because she is taking the unyielding position that his thinking is totally inaccurate and without merit. And as the argument drags on, we can see that this couple will never reach any kind of compromise much less a resolution if they continue to communicate in this destructive pattern.

WHAT WE CAN LEARN FROM THEM

If we are honest with ourselves, there's probably not one of us who hasn't engaged in an argument using the same tactic. When we feel strongly about something, it's hard to hold our tongues. Especially when we feel that the other person is biased in their thinking. However, this is exactly why we need to STOP and really LISTEN to the other person.

The most important point is that there is a problem which needs resolution. If it's left unresolved, it's going to eat away at the couple until their relationship begins to suffer.

A BETTER APPROACH

If you are aware that during arguments you constantly interrupt, the FIRST thing you'll need to practice is to keep your thoughts to yourself until the other person has finished his statement. No matter how much you want to cut in because you feel he's totally off base, don't! Let him voice his thoughts while you make an effort to really listen and try to understand his point of view. Then go ahead and state your opinion. Keep in mind that you are working together to remedy a problem. Always remember, YOU ARE NOT EACH OTHER'S ENEMY. You are two people who simply VIEW A PROBLEM DIFFERENTLY.

Let's look at how this problem could have been handled differently, keeping the points we discussed in mind:

SHE: "Dawn really wants to have her own car. I know she hasn't shown too much maturity in the past, but she's made some recent efforts which show some growth. Her grades have been very good, she wants to apply for a part-time job, and she's been helping more around the house."

HE: "Well, I think she's got to show more than that."

SHE: "O.K., what else do you expect from her?"

HE: "She'll have to be more careful with our car and show me a better level of maturity."

51

SHE: "I'm not sure exactly what you mean. Can you tell me more specifically what it would take for her to prove her maturity to you?"

HE: "I think she drives too fast and is too reckless. She doesn't pick up a thing in her room. She doesn't seem to respect any authority."

SHE: " Well, if she enrolled in a driving course at school and learned to be a more careful driver and consistently kept her room clean, would that help change your attitude?"

HE: "Probably. But I'd want to watch her driving carefully over the next few months. And she'll need to respect my opinions on things a lot more than she's doing."

SHE: "Fair enough. Why don't you sit down with her and tell her how she can go about showing you more respect? I know she's willing. I think you'll also see a change in her attitude."

HE: "I'll talk to her this afternoon. I think we need to discuss what our expectations are of each other at this point. If I feel she is truly willing to make an effort, then I'll take that into consideration."

This scenario demonstrated how much easier the problem gets solved when you aren't invalidating the other. These were the things that were done differently:

1. The wife did not offer excuses for the daughter.

2. She showed respect for her husband's feelings by not interrupting him.

3. She asked his opinion about what their daughter needed to do in order to take more responsibility.

4. The wife did not attempt to invalidate the husband's opinions.

5. The wife accepted the compromise of driving school without further protest.

This kind of interaction is not easy to accomplish. It takes hard work and self-control. MAKE A RULE BETWEEN YOU THAT ONE PARTY MUST LET THE OTHER FINISH BEFORE STATING HIS OPINIONS. If you learn to incorporate the above procedure in your discussions, you'll see how much more constructive your arguments will become. You will also find that it's a lot easier to reach a compromise or resolve the problem completely when you discuss matters in a spirit of real cooperation.

* * * THE SCREAMER * * *

Oh boy. We have all been guilty of this at times. Shouting happens when we feel like the other person is just not getting what we have to say. So we say it louder and louder. We are angry and it's a natural reaction to our anger. But what does it really accomplish? Nothing. It just makes the other person get angrier and louder. Then the argument dissolves into one big screaming match where neither party hears or understands a word the other says. Nothing is accomplished but bad feelings.

So what do you do? When you feel the urge to start yelling that is exactly the time to LOWER your voice dramatically. This forces the other person to become quiet to hear what you're saying and in doing so, it automatically lowers the vitriolic of the discussion. Believe me, it works. If you start doing this on a regular basis, you will see great results. We are all so sensitized to shouting. You hated it when you were a kid and your parents yelled at you. And you hate it as an adult. But unfortunately, it's the easiest trap of all to fall into. Lowering your voice and speaking without venom in your tone will take a lot of self–control, but the results are amazing. You will turn down the jets to a point where you can actually process what the other person has to say. If you need a time out to get it together enough to do this, then take it. But be sure to let your other half know it's a time-out and not that you're just walking away.

I saw a psychologist use this technique on a talk show and the results were amazing. There was a family who were just sitting there screaming at one another. No one was listening to anyone else. And they had been arguing this way for years. It was no wonder the family was a total non-functioning group of angry individuals. Then the psychologist started talking to them in a very low and controlled tone. At first, nobody listened to her. But then to my amazement, after about three minutes the family started to pipe down so they could hear her. She instructed them to start dealing that way with each other. And lo and behold! Within minutes they were actually LISTENING to each other. It was the first step that had to be taken in a long process of healing. The results were so dramatic that the audience sat in stunned silence.

It will work for you. So start incorporating this technique right away into your own interactions. It's going to make a huge difference.

* * * THE "THROW IN THE KITCHEN SINK" FIGHTER * * *

There are a lot of people who argue by throwing in all kinds of non-related issues from the past or present. This technique serves no useful purpose and all it does is cloud the real issues. It makes the two people involved in the argument get sidetracked and waste all their time fighting about completely irrelevant issues. Not only is it infuriating to the other person, but it blocks any chance of resolving the issue at hand.

Why do some people do this? There are many reasons. One is because there's still a lot of unresolved issues between them that are very much alive and festering. So they'll use the current forum to resurrect them, attempting to get some kind of resolution. Another reason is that the party bringing them up feels they are relevant to the present argument. And they may or may not be, but it doesn't matter. Throwing up past problems will make the other person feel like he's being assaulted on all sides. Shut-down occurs because they feel that they are being thrust into a NO-WIN SITUATION. And the truth is–they are.

Do you find yourself arguing this way? I think that women tend to argue this way more often than men. How many times have you heard a man say that his wife remembers every word of every argument they had 20 years ago, and she drags it up and throws it into the current argument? How can you avoid arguing this way?

1. *DISCUSS ONE ISSUE AT A TIME. IF YOU FEEL THAT THERE ARE OLD ISSUES WHICH WEREN'T RESOLVES TO YOUR SATISFACTION, SAVE THEM FOR A SEPARATE FORUM.*

2. *MAKE A PACT THAT NEITHER OF YOU WILL BRING UP ANY OTHER SUBJECT THAN THE ONE YOU'RE DISCUSSING.*

3. *ASK YOURSELF THIS QUESTION. AM I UPSET ABOUT THIS ISSUE OR AM I STILL MAD AT HIM FOR SOMETHING ELSE?*

4. *IF YOU FIND YOURSELF WANDERING ONTO ANOTHER TOPIC, APOLOGIZE FOR BRINGING IT UP AND GET ON WITH THE ORIGINAL ISSUE.*

5. *SET UP A WEEKLY OR MONTHLY DISCUSSION TIME SPECIFICALLY FOR DISCUSSING PAST UNRESOLVED ISSUES.*

* * * *THE #*X**!OX-! FIGHTER* * * *

Swearing, cuss words, and profanity often seem to be the most prevalent words you hear in arguments. Come on! We are all guilty of it. It's awfully hard not to let them slip out when we are really steamed!! But ask yourself these questions: "Does foul language ever help in any way to get a problem solved? Does it get his attention in a positive way?" Or does it act like a little arrow that sticks into the other person's flesh and further infuriates him. Swearing constitutes a personal attack. The vulgarities eventually go from being thrown into the fight to becoming directly attached to the person. Then it makes him go on the DEFENSIVE.

It's ugly and uncivilized when you allow your forum to degenerate into a filthy, name-calling battle of words. Rise above this temptation.

SUGGESTION BOX

1. MAKE A PACT THAT NEITHER OF YOU ARE GOING TO USE VULGAR LANGUAGE OR SWEAR DIRECTLY AT THE OTHER DURING THE DISCUSSION.

2. IF YOU LET SOME VULGARITIES SLIP OUT, THE ARGUMENT SHOULD STOP IMMEDIATELY UNTIL THERE IS AN APOLOGY FROM THE OFFENDER.

3. CONTINUE ON ONLY IF THERE IS NO ATMOSPHERE OF NASTINESS. IF THERE IS, TAKE A TIME-OUT AND COOL OFF.

4. KEEP YOUR CONCERNS AND FEELINGS FOCUSED ON THE PROBLEM, NOT ON EACH OTHER.

5. MAKE A CONCERTED EFFORT TO WORK ON YOUR SELF-CONTROL IN AN ATTEMPT TO KEEP THE DISCUSSION FAIR AND WITHOUT RANCOR.

---

* * * THE THREATENER * * *

Couples should always strive to create an environment where each can voice his complaints without fear of reprisal or rejection. When you think you are losing an argument, it is very easy to get into a pattern of trying to intimidate your partner by threatening to leave the marriage or the relationship. When tempers flare, neither is listening to the other, and you feel like you're losing ground, a common tactic is to say something like this:

"Well, if you really feel this way about me, then we'd just better call it quits right now. If you think so little of me, it's time for me to leave."

And very often it works—for the moment. The other person has seen he's pushed too hard and becomes afraid you'll carry out your threat. So he backs off. However, this is a case of winning the battle but losing the war. The threats end the argument but the issue has not been resolved. And each time this tactic is repeated, it builds up walls of isolation more and more. Resentment and confusion ensue. It sets the stage for a spouse to become extremely reluctant to discuss any further problems which arise. So issue after issue goes unresolved and smolders between them. This is another relationship killer. Couples have got to make a safe arena for discussion, otherwise communication will die a quick death.

Here's another pact you need to make with your spouse if you find that this is a tactic you both use. *Promise each other that no matter how heated things get or no matter how severely you disagree, you will NEVER threaten to leave.* Keep the sanctity of your marriage out of it. You are arguing over issues or situations that need resolutions. Threatening to leave the marriage will never bring about the permanent resolution of anything. Make it a cardinal rule that this type of threat will be strictly out of bounds.

Another variation of this type of behavior is when you try to get even with the other person by making them suffer over an unrelated incident. For example, he may complain that you aren't treating his mother with enough kindness. You fight about it and threaten to leave. The argument abruptly ends without resolution. Then two weeks later when your mother is visiting, he acts coldly towards HER to get even with YOU. So what was accomplished here? Nothing but negatives. Your mother is confused and hurt and you are furious at him because you know what he was trying to do. He is still seething at you because he felt you were unresponsive to his original complaints. Now you've got a web of stuff to clear up instead of just the original issue. So you can see how this kind of behavior leads to more problems than you expected. Besides, it will continue to infiltrate other aspects of your relationship.

The practice of getting even requires forethought. You plan to behave a certain way in order to teach someone a lesson. It would be far more constructive to channel your energies into positive measures for resolution. So when you are considering this type of behavior:

1. *REVIEW THE ORIGINAL PROBLEM IN YOUR MIND. IDENTIFY WHAT WASN'T RESOLVES AND DISCUSS IT WITH YOUR PARTNER. TRY TO GET A RESOLUTION AND THEN DROP IT.*

2. *IF YOU STILL FEEL LIKE GETTING EVEN, THEN THE PROBLEM WASN'T RESOLVED TO YOUR SATISFACTION. DON'T SCHEME ABOUT TEACHING A LESSON TO THE OFFENDING PARTY. PUT YOUR ENERGIES INTO CREATING A DIFFERENT APPROACH IN ATTACKING THE PROBLEM.*

3. *THINK ABOUT THE RAMIFICATIONS OF A PLAN TO GET EVEN. IS IT REALLY GOING TO SOLVE THE ORIGINAL PROBLEM? THINK ABOUT WHAT FUTURE PROBLEMS AND ILL-WILL YOUR ACTIONS COULD CAUSE IF YOU CARRY OUT YOUR MISGUIDED INTENTIONS.*

* * * THE MARATHON ARGUMENT * * *

Arguments drag on for hours when:

1. UNRELATED ISSUES are continually being introduced
2. Neither party is LISTENING to the other
3. Both parties are unwilling to COMPROMISE on any level

Sometimes couples get sidetracked and trapped in an argument which is taking too many wrong turns and covering too many non–relevant issues. This type of argument can drag on for hours. If this is happening in your relationship, it's easy to correct. Make a "15 Minute" rule that you will both adhere to. *If the argument is dragging on past 15 minutes with no end in sight, you'll need to stop.* Give yourselves a break for a few minutes, or a few hours or even a day before resuming the discussion.

What happens with long arguments is that they go WAY PAST THE POINT of constructive action and become totally counter-productive. They exhaust and depress the participants. Neither is willing to compromise and expects to have an outcome which is 100% their own way. And when this doesn't happen, nobody wins and nothing gets resolved. Stick to the 15 minute rule and in your quiet time, reflect on what was really being said on both sides of the discussion. Try to analyze objectively where you were both at fault in not completing and resolving the issue. Then when you begin anew, you should be in a more serene mood and have a greater willingness to work at reaching a compromise on the issue.

LEARNING TO SAY I'M SORRY

During a disagreement, if one party expects the other to apologize for his behavior and doesn't hear it, he will often keep the battle raging on until he gets one. But sadly, with some people this will never happen because *they would rather die than APOLOGIZE.* It's a psychological thing with some people. They think that apologizing is the same as admitting guilt and having to take responsibility for everything that occurred.

Most of the time it's the buttons we push in the other person that escalate the argument rather than the issues themselves. *I am NOT suggesting that an apology will ALWAYS end or solve an argument.* However, it does one very powerful thing. It lets the other person know that you are willing to accept some responsibility for the problem and respect their feelings enough to admit it.

So, *if you ARE AT FAULT in a specific situation, APOLOGIZE for it. Take that responsibility.* If he was mad at you because you promised to be on time and you were an hour late—admit it. Don't defend it or excuse it!

"Honey, I apologize for being an hour late. There were reasons for it, but I know that's beside the point. I let you down and I am really very sorry for doing that."

That's it! Now that wasn't so bad was it? I'll tell you a little secret that works every time. *When you offer a SINCERE apology (no sarcasm, no attitude) it ends the battle.* When you accept responsibility, it's over. There's nothing else left to apologize for. It's empowering! By the same token, *spouses have to learn to ACCEPT AN APOLOGY GRACIOUSLY and LET IT END there.* When the apology is not just a manipulative tool to get the person off the hook but is done with sincerity, then there's nothing left to disagree about. It's so easy to say, *"Honey, I know you feel bad about the way you spoke to me and I accept your apology."*

* * * THE INVALIDATOR * * *

There are those people who can be described as "never cutting another person a break." This happens when one person prolongs an argument by telling the other that he has "no right to feel that way" or by saying, "your thinking is all wrong" or similar inflammatory statements. The point is that you have no right to place your expectations about how another person should feel or react on them. It may certainly not be how you feel about it, but the fact is that everyone has a right to own his own opinions even when they differ from yours. By stating an immediate invalidation of the other person, you are in effect, closing all channels for further communication. Very often the other person will respond by saying "Well, then there's no reason to continue this discussion. It's obvious that we think differently and will never reach an understanding."

To avoid this trap, it's important to learn how to VALIDATE the other person. You can say something like this:

"I do not agree with your thinking on this matter but I respect the way you feel about it. Now, let me explain how my thinking is different from your's and let's see if we can come to some mutual understanding."

Even if you think he's nuts, isn't this a better way to proceed? At least you are showing respect and a willingness to come to some meeting of the minds. It puts you both in a more open frame of mind to come to an agreement. Let's face it. We are all individuals with very different feelings and opinions. That's why disagreements arise all the time in the course of a relationship. But it's a big mistake to just assume the self-serving opinion that he is crazy and has no justification in feeling the way he does. This is the same thing as saying you have no respect for who he is or what he is saying.

Following the same logic, it's important during the course of an argument to validate each other's thinking when you do agree. If he makes a good point in an argument, give him his due. Say: *"You know something, honey? I agree with what you said on that issue and I want you to know it. You made a very valid point."* Then when a portion of the argument arises where you totally disagree with him, he won't be so defensive. He'll be a lot calmer and more open to listen to your point of view. This is a very smart way to handle discussions. And when you begin incorporating this technique into your interactions you will see that it tends to work minor miracles.

* * * FROM ARGUMENT TO ARGUMENT TO ARGUMENT * * *

There are couples who argue over an issue, bring it to a resolution and then quickly find a new issue to argue about. So it seems like they never stop arguing. Why does this happen? Usually it happens because the couple is not really arguing about issues but rather because they don't feel like they're loved or supported by the other person. So they walk around with a kind discontentment hidden just below the surface. And it takes very little provocation to bring it back up to the surface. So when a new issue comes up, they are quick to anger. However, after that problem gets resolved, they still don't feel quite right about it. They don't feel the relief or final resolution they think they should be feeling. And after each successive issue is solved, they are baffled because they don't feel any closer to each other!

GETTING DOWN TO IT

This is what will keep occurring until they realize what is actually at the heart of the matter. And when they begin to peel back those layers and recognize that they are feeling so unappreciated and unloved that they want to lash out in anger against each other, then they can change things. If this is becoming a pattern of behavior with you and your spouse, take the necessary time to analyze what's going on inside you. And when you get to the bottom of what you are really disturbed about, then tell him.

You might say, *"You know what I discovered today? I discovered that we're arguing about one issue after another because I don't feel loved and appreciated by you. This is what's REALLY bothering me a lot more than the issues themselves. And most likely you're doing the same thing. So let's talk about it and try to get to a place where we are meeting each other's needs and making each other feel appreciated again. And when we can do this, it's going to put an end to our frequent arguments."*

STRIPPING OFF THE LAYERS

The following scenario shows a couple arguing from their anger only. They never get past this level and down to what's really bothering them. It serves to illustrate the point that when couples don't examine their feelings in-depth during a disagreement, those untapped feelings just serve as a spark for a future argument. In this scenario, the wife wants to get a job and the husband doesn't want her to. They have argued about it in the past many times.

HE: "Why are you always bringing this up? I told you a hundred times I don't want you to go to work. Your place is at home here with me and the kids. We don't need the money, that's for sure!"

SHE: "Just listen to you!! My place? It sounds like you consider me to be a possession who has no right to her own opinions. How insulting!!"

HE: "Why do you twist everything? It's those stupid women's libber friends of your's who poison your mind! You're making this into a much bigger thing than it has to be!"

SHE: "Oh sure. Now it's all my fault! If I would just keep my mouth shut and have no opinions or thoughts, everything would be perfectly all right with you."

HE: "You're impossible to talk to. I have to go to work." (He leaves feeling angry and she is furious)

WHAT'S UNDERNEATH

This couple is arguing from their anger only. They are frustrated because each feels the other will never see his point of view. They are weary of getting into this argument that has no resolution because it always leaves a trail of bitterness and bad feelings behind. But their real problem isn't that she wants to work. Yet, neither is getting past his own anger and conveying to the other what's REALLY troubling him. If they could peel back the anger, there would be a lot of hurt underneath. He's hurt because he thinks that she isn't happy with her role as a wife and mother. He is also hurt because she views him as a monstrous chauvinist which he feels he isn't. She's hurt because she feels he doesn't value and respect her as an intelligent person. She is also hurt because he thinks she can be so easily influenced by her friends and is not capable of coming to her own decisions.

And when we peel back another layer what we find is that they are both AFRAID. He's afraid that he could potentially lose her. He might be fantasizing that she could potentially meet another man in the workplace who will fulfill her needs better than he can. She's afraid that she will have to remain stifled at home, and never get to utilize her brain and talents. She's afraid she will become so resentful against him for not allowing her to work that she will ultimately begin to hate him.

JUST SAY IT

Most arguments have elements of hurt and fear buried underneath. So the next time you are hurling anger back and forth at each other, *take the time to identify what is UNDERNEATH your anger. Then communicate it. Tell each other that you're really hurt and WHY you are hurt.* And after you have expressed the hurt, see what else you're feeling. Ask yourself what you're afraid of–and tell him. This is what's known as *working through your anger.* And it's crucial that you are able to do this if you are ever going to reach a lasting resolution where peace and harmony can be restored to your relationship.

Practice going through this thought process every time something comes up that bothers you. It's a very healthy way to deal with your feelings because you aren't avoiding any of them. Instead, you're going through all the layers and cleaning it through to the core. You will feel an enormous emotional as well as physical release when you start doing it. You will also find that your discussions will become shorter and get resolved more easily without all the emotional bruising that comes with the anger.

LONG TERM RESULTS

The main message of this chapter is that destructive arguing will kill the passion in a relationship faster than anything else because it builds up long-term resentments. And resentment builds emotional walls which are erected in an attempt to further insulate a person from future hurts. However, the danger lies in the fact that it also numbs a person to positive feelings like joy and love. You cannot reach a person emotionally who has a wall built around himself. And this will eventually squeeze all the sexual spark and passion out of a marriage or long-term relationship.

I found it interesting that many of the women who were in long-term marriages said they still loved their spouse, but very few used the phrase that they were still in love with them. And believe me, there is a vast difference. It's like the difference between cuddling and actual intercourse. People who have years of unresolved problems between them lose their emotional anchor with each other. They are no longer soul-mates. They no longer put each other first in everything they do. Why? Because the unresolved resentment towards each other has literally robbed them of their love and passion. I go back to my original premise: *It is impossible to make passionate love with somebody you are constantly mad at or resent deeply.* The two exclude all sexual feelings. And this is especially true with females because of the way we view sex, itself. We have to respect, adore and love the soul of our men to have wonderful, fulfilling sex.

That's why this chapter is so important. And what it all comes down to is that it's not the argument, per se, that kills feelings. It's the years of unresolved arguments that leave each party feeling like he or she has been ignored, disrespected, unloved and unimportant. Both parties feel like the other has always gotten his way and the satisfaction they should have felt never materialized for them. This is why the passion is dead. This is why you cringe when he touches you. This is why you are constantly making excuses why you don't want to make love. You basically resent him for the years of unresolved and bitter fights.

Is it hopeless? No! But you'll need to frequently review the "POSITIVE STEPS FOR BETTER COMMUNICATION" in the cut-out section to follow. Be honest with yourself. Identify and admit what negative roles you have been playing. And when you have truly understood how destructive those old negative ways of communication have been, use the techniques we have discussed to begin changing your method of interaction with your spouse. These techniques work! But be creative. Everybody's situation is a little bit different. Once you've understood the principles and how they work, try a variation of your own. Sit down and really think about how you argue or don't argue. Identify your particular interactions that have been tremendously adverse to your communication and relationship in general. Discuss them with your spouse. Then institute your own rules together.

Explain to him that you are beginning to understand that your lack of passion has been a result of these things over a period of time. Tell him how much you want to get back "on track" in all areas of your relationship ESPECIALLY your sexual relationship. No man is going to turn away from that. I know that most men will be extremely happy and excited about hearing you say that. They will be only too willing to cooperate with you as you attempt to recapture the old sexual passion you once shared. Be positive and keep working at it together. You are going to be amazed at how close you will become when the curtain of resentment is lifted by using these techniques to improve your communication. It's going to expand into every facet of your relationship in a healing and healthy way.

RECAP: SOME POSITIVE STEPS FOR BETTER COMMUNICATION

If you are having difficulties in your relationship because of frequent and unresolved arguments, I have prepared this CUT-OUT SECTION, listing steps you can follow to have calmer and more productive discussions with your mate. Refer to it often and especially before attempting to discuss a troublesome issue with him. It will help to keep you focused and to avoid the common pitfalls which lead to destructive arguments.

1. LISTEN TO WHAT THE OTHER PERSON IS SAYING. -Don't constantly interrupt. -Don't spend your time writing internal scripts for your rebuttal. You'll miss hearing valuable information that could be used to resolve the problem.

2. ATTACK THE PROBLEM NOT THE PERSON. -Tell him it's his BEHAVIOR that's troubling you not him as a person. -Don't use foul language. -Don't belittle or call him stupid. -Remind him that you love him but disagree with how he's ACTING.

3. DON'T TRY TO INVALIDATE HIM. -Give him credit for his valid points. -Keep your comments positive. -Try to put yourself in his place to really understand what he's feeling.

4. DON'T SHOUT AND SCREAM. -Make yourself remain calm. -Take "time-outs" when needed to de-escalate the argument. -Stop being defensive.

5. BE SPECIFIC IN WHAT YOU'RE ARGUING ABOUT. -Don't bring up matters that happened in the past. -Don't throw in other unrelated issues into the fray. -Try very hard to keep both of you attuned to the specific problem at hand.

6. LIMIT THE ARGUMENT TO 15 MINUTES. -Stop and go back when you have calmed down and analyzed the problem. -Be succinct–don't say the same things over and over again or try to keep making the same point. -If either concedes on a particular aspect of the argument, acknowledge it and move on.

7. LEARN TO APOLOGIZE. -Accept responsibility and apologize when you are at fault. -Learn to graciously accept his apology and move on. -Become aware that an apology is the best and quickest way to HEAL a relationship and use it often.

8. LEARN TO FORGIVE. -The act of forgiving is the greatest empowerment you have.-If you remain angry and resentful, the relationship will be stifled and eventually disintegrate. -Remember the Golden Rule, "Do Unto Others As You Would Have Them Do Unto You," it's one of life's most valuable tenets to practice.

9. DO NOT PLACE EXPECTATIONS ON THE OTHER PERSON.-Expectations will set you up for failure every time.-When you expect nothing, everything else becomes a pleasant bonus. -Remember that you are individuals with different thoughts, ideals and opinions. Don't superimpose yours on him!

10. SET UP SCHEDULED TIMES FOR DISCUSSIONS. -The environment will be calmer and less combative. -You can head off a lot of potential fights this way. -You can solve a lot more things when you aren't furious with each other.

11. WORK THROUGH YOUR ANGER. -Ask yourself if you are really hurt instead of angry–and then express that hurt. -Once you have identified the hurt, go deeper and ask yourself what you're afraid of. Then express your fears. -End each discussion by telling each other how much you love them. Then apologize for any hurt you have inflicted. -Keep all arguments out of the bedroom!

12. WRITE A LETTER TO YOUR SPOUSE. -Take time to write a letter expressing all the levels of your feelings. -Tell your spouse how you plan to correct the problem by working through your feelings. -Tell him what you want for the future in terms of there solution of the problem.

13. TAKE THE TIME TO RESOLVE ISSUES WHILE THEY'RE SMALL –Schedule regular discussions to specifically air out the little things that are bothering you. -Don't keep stuffing your annoyance. You'll be resentful and carry around that unresolved anger. It's baggage you don't need. -Remember that little issues become big issues which can do a lot more damage and at some point become irreparable.

CHAPTER 5

THE KIDS

THE IDEAL

I believe that an environment of mutual nurturing should be firmly established in a marriage before adding children to the mix. The responsibility of raising children and the time and effort you will put into nurturing them is overwhelming. And if a husband and wife are not fully practiced in nurturing each other, it's never going to be established once the kids arrive into the family. The kind of love that children give to their parents is unconditional and extremely deep in nature. *But love from your children should never replace the need for love and friendship that a husband and wife should have for each other.* And the danger in having kids before that foundation is established is that it often does replace that marital need.

Unfortunately, there are a lot of marriages which take place because a child is on the way. And there are more, still, in which the kids come within the first year or two. And in these cases, it often prevents any chance the couple has of building a mutual foundation between themselves. In many of these marriages, the focus of their love is transferred to the children immediately and the couple never has the chance to experience it between them. Then they find themselves in a situation where one or both spouses complains that their sex life is terrible or non-existent. In this chapter, we will explore how couples can intentionally and unintentionally allow their children to put a damper on their sex lives.

AFTER THE BABY COMES

After the baby arrives, there are many physical and emotional factors which act to decrease a woman's sexual appetite. Hormonal changes can definitely play a role in decreasing a woman's desire to have sex. This is a normal occurrence. Factors such as nursing a baby and post-partum fluxes in hormones often act in combination, producing added feelings of exhaustion and depression. So it is not surprising to hear these women complain that they're "too exhausted" from their hectic schedule of taking care of the baby to have sex. The problem then becomes cyclical: the less sex you have the less you begin to desire it. So the wife begins to constantly put her husband off. She may even feel like her breasts belong to the baby now and are *off limits* to her husband. Also many women get into the habit of putting the baby in bed with them because they don't want to keep getting up during the night for breast or bottle feeding.

The normal reaction of most husbands is to become more sexually demanding because he feels like he has to compete with the baby for his wife's body and her attention. If this situation is left to fester, it is going to put a definite rift in the marriage. An ongoing competition will be set up between father and child which further widens the emotional distance between husband and wife. This is a very common situation for new parents to fall into. And it undermines the spousal relationship because the wife is so fulfilled with the love and joy of her child that she closes her eyes to what's happening between her and her husband.

AVOIDING THE TRAP

If you can identify yourself in this scenario, then it's time for remedial action. The first and foremost thing to remember is that a healthy and fulfilling sexual life in your marriage should be a top priority. Sexual and emotional bonding are the cornerstones of every marriage and no marriage is going to survive without it. It's every husband and wife's right to expect it and work towards achieving it.

So it is especially incumbent on a wife that she pay attention to the sexual needs of her husband. If she has always done this before the baby came, then chances are she will do so afterwards. But, if you get into the pattern of continually *putting sex off*, you'll need to examine your motivations closely. You will have to come to the realization that refusing him indefinitely is going to produce some serious consequences. He may eventually look for an affair to fulfill his needs or in the most extreme case, leave you. Here are some of the "reasons" that many women gave for continually postponing sex:

1. EXHAUSTION

♥ *"He just doesn't understand how exhausted I am. I don't feel like making love at midnight after I've spent a grueling day with the baby."*

THE REMEDY

Okay, for the moment, let's accept this as a valid excuse. New moms are often physically and emotionally drained at the end of the day. However, exhaustion shouldn't put your sex life in limbo for months or years. The answer is that you'll need to reschedule your sex life. If bedtime is the worst time for sex, than get creative. Put the baby to bed by 7 P.M. and allow an hour or so for alone time with your husband. Forget the laundry, the bottles and all the rest of it for a while. You know perfectly well that you will get these chores done later anyway. And if you have to put the laundry off for one more day, so what? Life as we know it on this planet will not end. Share a dinner alone with your husband. It doesn't have to be gourmet with candles–just a simple dinner ALONE WITH HIM. Talk and re-bond. Go cuddle and then make love. Make a habit of this. Do it once, twice or three times a week, or whatever fulfills both of you. There are no set rules–*what you both agree on IS THE RULE.*

If you have other young children to contend with, put them in bed by 7:30 or 8:30 P.M. This is an appropriate bedtime for them. If you allow your kids to run you ragged until 10 or 11 P.M. every night, YOU ARE CREAT-ING YOUR OWN PROBLEMS! Children can be regimented to have reasonable bedtimes. It's not only best for you, but also best for them as well.

During the weekends GET A BABYSITTER! Of course you are going to be particular about who stays with your child and you should be. Maybe you'll prefer that a family member watch the kids. But if you can't always get one, then you'll need to invest some time into searching for a person you trust who will be available. Some women do a "swap" night with their girlfriends when money is a problem. They schedule times when they will take each others kids to help out. This works well for many women. But the most ridiculous and self-defeating thing I have heard many women say is, "I would NEVER leave my kids with a babysitter. There's no one I would trust leaving my kids with." I think this is just plain stupid. All couples deserve some free time to keep nurturing their marital relationships. If I hear a woman making this kind of a statement, it tells me something. It tells me that she really doesn't want to be alone with her husband. And that's another problem we'll discuss later. The point is that there are always solutions to the exhaustion problem if you really want to find one. Take a nap when the baby does to be more refreshed at night. Remember when you were dating and you both found any way possible to be together all the time? There wasn't any situation you couldn't creatively solve in order to be together. And after you have established a regular pattern of nurturing each other again, then you will look forward to having your sexual time together. But don't let it slide until it's beyond repair. Pretend you are still dating!

2. DEMANDING BABY

♥ *"I have to put the baby in bed with us or else I'd never get any rest. He wakes up every two to three hours, and if I had to keep running into his room, I'd be up all night."*

THE REMEDY

Babies can be put on a schedule like anyone else. If the baby is in bed with you, he will soon learn that every time he cries, you will immediately pick him up and hold him. He will get used to this situation and have problems being weaned back into his crib. The answer is to keep the baby out of your bed in the first place. For one thing, it's far more dangerous to have an infant between two adults than tucked snugly away in his own crib. There is always the danger that a sleeping adult could roll over on him or partially cover his airway with a blanket or a body part. A baby or young child needs to become familiar with the security of his own bed. Naturally, in the first year the baby will wake up crying to be fed during the night, depending on his feeding schedule. But even if you put the crib in the room with you until he sleeps through the night, it's do-able.

GET THE BABY OUT OF YOUR BED RIGHT NOW if that's what you're doing. It may take a few weeks of him fussing and crying for a few stretches of time, but it isn't impossible to get him on a regular schedule. Talk to your pediatrician about it. Talk with girlfriends or mothers who have successfully formed a reasonable schedule with their kids' bed and feeding times. Listen and learn from the success of others. But don't wait too long. It will be a hundred times harder to try to retrain a four or six month old than a six week old.

3. THE OLDER CHILD WHO SLEEPS IN YOUR BED

♥ *"We allowed our baby to sleep with us for the first year. Now he is two and screams so much when we try to put him in his own room, we can't figure out what else to do."*

MAKE HIS ROOM APPEALING

I can never stress this enough. CHILDREN HAVE NO PLACE IN THEIR PARENTS' BEDS. Your bed should be for two married adults only. It is the one place of sanctuary where you can talk, play, make love and emotionally bond without interruption. Take that away and the relationship is headed for rough waters. Take the child and put him in his bed. Yes, he is going to fuss for a week or two. But if you give in and carry him back to your bed, he has accomplished what he wanted to do. Naturally, it isn't the child's fault. You created this situation. And by the same token, it's up to you to change it. Do you expect to forgo sex for the next five years? I don't know what adults are thinking when they allow this situation to be created. The only conclusion I can draw is that one or both of the parents is using the child to avoid having physical contact with the other. Anything else doesn't make sense. And if you are avoiding each other, ask yourselves this question? How long do you think it will take before you are so physically and emotionally estranged that your marriage will be a mere shell? Any couple who willingly allows their marriage to degenerate this way has serious problems underlying their basic relationship. And it's going to take counseling and a lot of work if both parties wish the marriage to heal and continue.

On the practical side, there's a lot of creative things you can do to make a child's room appealing. Little boys love those beds shaped like race cars or fire engines. Also, a comforter with his or her favorite cartoon characters on it will make a child feel *at home* in his bed. Teddy bear shaped pillows, colorful nite–lights, and "glo-in-the-dark" stars and moons on the ceiling will all help to create a pleasant, warm and safe atmosphere where he can enjoy being in his own bed. Establish a 15 minute "story-time" period where you stay with the child until he gets sleepy. But then when it's over, the child must accept the fact that you are going to leave the room. Don't keep running back every five minutes if he starts to fuss. This will establish a pattern where he knows his fussing will get results. It's just a matter of establishing a routine he's comfortable with and STICKING TO IT.

4. POST-PARTUM LOSS OF SEX DRIVE

♥ *"I knew this problem wasn't all in my head. I experienced a marked loss in my sex drive for about a year after the baby arrived. I just didn't seem to feel that natural 'urge' for sex, and when I did have sex the feelings weren't as intense or pleasurable as before. Thank goodness after about a year, things returned to normal."*

The bad news is that a decreased sex drive is a very common reaction after childbirth which many women have to face. The good news is that *it WILL NOT last forever.* The major hormonal and physical changes which take place during the nine months of pregnancy take time to reverse themselves post-partum. It takes months or even up to a year for that to happen. You may have an episiotomy incision that has to heal, your birth canal muscles have been temporarily stretched to accommodate the baby during delivery, and you are secreting hormones which affect lactation and the act of breast feeding keeps those hormones stimulated until you stop. These are just a few of the apparent changes pregnancy and delivery will bring about. And they do affect your sex drive. Hormonal changes are real and have a tremendous physical impact on womens' bodies. That's why women are sick and tired of hearing misinformed men make statements like "it's all in your head."

It is important for a woman NOT to place any pre-conceptions or expectations upon herself during her pregnancy and post-partum months. Every woman reacts differently to her own hormonal changes and to the different levels of stress after the baby arrives. So you'll need to just take it as it comes and adjust accordingly. And the degree of success in how you handle it will be affected greatly by your ability to communicate with your spouse. Remember, he is not a mind reader. You'll need to explain your feelings openly and completely to him so he doesn't take it personally.

THE REMEDY

Let's take this step by step. Okay, you have temporarily lost some of your sex drive. First of all, discuss it with your gynecologist. He or she is a professional who can best assess your physical and emotional state. On your post-partum check-ups, he will make sure your body is healing normally and there aren't any physical problems interfering with sex. After any physical problems have been ruled out, he can counsel you using the expertise he's gained from years of treating similar problems of new mothers. *Don't be shy about telling him what's going on with you.* Believe me, he will have answers and advice to any of your questions. These specialists have HEARD IT ALL over the years!

Once you know your body is functioning normally, you can begin to work with your emotions. *Sit down with your husband and explain how you are feeling.* Tell him that your doctor assures you that your lowered sexual feelings are normal and temporary, but you are both going to have to deal with them. Naturally with the demands of a new baby, your sex life is going to slow down for a while. But your husband has to be reassured that it has nothing to do with your love for him. Don't assume he will automatically know this because he won't. It is entirely normal for him to feel some degree of competition with the baby. When you work at keeping your emotional bonds with him as strong as before the baby came, it will also make the whole situation much easier for him to cope with.

And even though you may feel a lot less like having sex, you have to realize that your sex life cannot come to an abrupt halt. You may require more foreplay, more cuddling or even just a lot more touching by him to get you in the mood. This is perfectly okay as long as you let HIM know.

It's really not that complicated. Men can be very understanding when they realize that it's not a personal thing. But it will take repeated communication and assurance to make sure no resentment creeps into the picture. You will find that this kind of two-way communication will generate the desired cooperation and support from your spouse. You may find that your sex life bounces back a lot faster and actually improves a great deal when both of your feelings are aired on a regular basis. Remember, it's an attitude of "we-ness" which gets results. And when there is love and understanding being freely exchanged, it's awfully hard for misunderstanding and resentment to come between you.

5. BODY IMAGE

♥ *"I hate the way my body looks now. Our baby is two months old and I am still flabby and paunchy. So far, I haven't been able to lose the extra 15 pounds I kept on after the baby was born. I don't feel sexy anymore and my self-esteem is suffering as much as our sex life."*

The way we feel about our own bodies has a tremendous bearing on our sexuality and therefore, a direct effect on our sexual desires. If we hate looking at our own body you can be sure we are assuming that our husband hates looking at it, too. Even though this may be the furthest thing from the truth, it's going to be nearly impossible for us to believe otherwise no matter how much we're told it isn't so. Loss of self-esteem is a very detrimental thing. It pervades every part of who we are and how we see ourselves as well as how it affects our relationships with others. If we hate ourselves, we are naturally going to be a lot more envious of others. It's such a destructive feeling that we cannot allow it to continue on without seriously damaging our relationship.

THE REMEDY

This woman clearly defined her problem. She's overweight and out of shape since the baby came. She has two choices:

1. Do nothing to correct the weight gain and continue to criticize herself until she stops having sex with her husband completely and endangers the relationship.

    OR

2. Set a goal for herself and begin dieting and exercising until she reaches it.

We are the only ones who can CONTROL our bodies. But you must remember, that if you GAIN weight, it is never beyond your power to LOSE it too. You can accomplish this goal by getting on a weight loss shape up program. And it is not easier said than done. It's a matter of setting priorities. We have all heard the oh so convenient excuses:

- I don't have the time to exercise–the baby takes all my time.
- It's hormonal–I can't lose the weight no matter what I do.
- Joining a gym is too expensive.
- It's too hard to cook regular meals for my family and separate diet meals for me.

And so on and so on. Well, it all boils down to the question of DO YOU WANT TO LOSE THE WEIGHT AND LOOK GOOD AGAIN OR NOT? And if you REALLY DO, then a program of diet and exercise is the ONLY WAY TO ACCOMPLISH IT!! The excuses are meaningless. You either DO it or YOU DON'T. And no– you don't have to join a gym to lose weight. If you have a VCR and $15 for a video, you are in business. There are dozens and dozens of exercise videos to choose from. You can do step-aerobics in a very small area of your home right in front of the TV. You can choose high or low-impact or any one of numerous programs. Try a couple different ones and then choose which one you like the most and STICK TO IT. But it has to be one in which you're going to work up a sweat. Don't kid yourself. To burn off calories, you will have to put a good deal of exertion into it. And you should exercise at least every other day. If you combine your exercise program with simply eating sensibly, you won't need a strict diet to follow. YOU WILL LOSE WEIGHT AND YOU WILL TONE UP THE FLABBY MUSCLES. It's no big mystery. It will happen!!

There are many exercise machines like the Nordic Track which can give fabulous results and can be purchased with regular monthly payments. A lot of people put them in front of the TV in their bedroom or den and watch soaps or their favorite show during a 30 to 45 minute workout. Others swear by rowing machines, stair–steppers or treadmills. They pop a few great tapes into their Walkmans and go-go-go for a half-hour or more while working out to an inspiring beat! Many couples set aside regular time periods, like after dinner, to take their walks for a mile or more. They enjoy the *togetherness* and how good in general, it makes them feel. Exercise has been proven to be one of the best natural mood elevators around.

If you find that you cannot motivate yourself at home alone, then join a club. Exercise club memberships are really not expensive anymore. Clubs run specials to get new members all the time. You can join one for as little as $100 to $200 a year and go everyday if you want. I am speaking from my own experience here. My club cost me $159 per year and when I'm not traveling for my work, I go EVERY DAY. I weigh less now than I did when I was in high school 30 years ago. It's a priority for me and you need to make it your priority too. I guarantee that when you begin dropping those pounds and toning up, your self-esteem will soar! You will be so pleased with the way you look that you'll want to treat yourself to a sexy teddy every month. And your sex life will resume with a vengeance! And the only "secret" is that it has GOT TO BE A PRIORITY for you.

Also, you'll be delighted with all the added benefits from a regular exercise regime. You'll have increased energy, better health, a robust immune system and a surge in self-esteem. And these are all the necessary ingredients for a healthy, fulfilling sex life. It's the best present you can ever give yourself. And even if you have heard it a thousand times before, it bears repeating–YOU ARE WORTH IT. Now believe it and get going!

AS THE KIDS GET OLDER

There is no doubt that as your children progress beyond infancy into toddlers and youngsters, the demands on you as parents don't lessen–they simply shift a bit. So all the suggestions about maintaining intimacy with your spouse will still apply later on in your life. In fact, there are going to be certain new factors you'll need to become aware of when attempting to keep that romantic bond with your spouse. A very common problem that interferes with intimacy and leads to emotional starvation in a marriage is when the parents over-glorify the children.

It may sound a bit ridiculous at first, but let me explain what's involved in this process. Maybe it would make more sense to re-phrase it by saying that many parents make the mistake of centering their whole universe around their kids. They allow the children to dictate the parents' schedules and change their marital habits to a point where it creates an unhealthy emotional climate between the couple. Here are some of the ways this can happen even when parents feel they have the best of intentions.

1. ALLOWING THE CHILD TO SLEEP IN THE SAME BED AS THE PARENTS FROM INFANCY UNTIL HE IS WELL PAST TODDLER AGE.

We discussed this before, but now I want to get to the root of this practice. To be completely honest, *every couple I've known who did this had serious problems in their marriage.*

What we have here is a kind of a "chicken or the egg" situation. Did putting the baby in bed with them cause the estrangement or was the estrangement already there? Usually, the case is that the estrangement was already present. The important thing to keep in mind is that being parents doesn't PRECLUDE you from also being LOVERS. Love cannot be "used up," but your time and your commitment to nurturing each other as spouses can. Naturally we all recognize the profound obligation we have as parents to make our children feel loved and secure. But we should never forget that WE HAVE THAT SAME OBLIGATION TO OUR SPOUSES AS WELL. And one should never overshadow the other.

2. ALLOWING THE KIDS TO INTERFERE WITH YOUR MARITAL NURTURING.

There are parents who insist on taking their kids to adult functions where children really don't belong. I, personally, have a big problem with this behavior. I have been out for the evening to dinner with adults and one couple will always bring their child along. And I always ask myself, "why do they do this?" The child obviously can't enjoy an all-adult dinner. The parents cannot freely interact with the other adults, much less each other, because they are giving most of their attention to the child. This is a prime example of over-glorifying a child. *You must make time for adult socialization WITHOUT the kids.* It is NORMAL and HEALTHY for a relationship. And couples who don't do this on a regular basis are putting a serious strain on their own relationship.

Adults need to have time to be adults and interact in an appropriate way. Couples need to feel like they are still "dating" in order to keep their passion alive no matter how old their kids are. Adults need sexual time, romantic time and time to converse and bond alone. And if we don't do this for ourselves and our marriages, we are going to drift apart from our spouses in many different ways. Remember the "How It Was" chapter? The dating couples made their "alone time" a priority above all else. It was the most direct way of maintaining their emotional closeness and this is what kept their passion cooking. Children should not put a stop to this practice. It is as important after 20 years of marriage as it was in the beginning of the relationship.

3. VERBALLY IDEALIZING THE CHILD

It is important to build a child's self-esteem by giving praise when appropriate. It's necessary for their emotional growth. In return, our children give us that unconditional love which contributes to our own self-esteem. This is all a normal part of parenting. However, when we idealize the child to the point that we get all our self-esteem from him and not from our spouses, it is seriously detrimental to our marital relationships.

We must always remember that we need to love our spouses in the same unconditional atmosphere as we do our kids. In our marital relationships, we should not overlook the need to give praise and see the best in our partners as we do with our children. We need that same self-esteem building approval from our partners in order to keep our focus of importance on them and the marriage. To replace this by allowing it to come solely from our children is a big mistake. This practice will lead to emotional starvation between the spouses in the marriage. Adults need to feel that they are still #1 with each other in their marital arenas. We need to keep nurturing our partner and letting him know how loved and important he is to us. It takes so little effort to say "I love you and couldn't live without you." It's this kind of bonding that has to be maintained in order to keep that old passion alive between us.

4. ALLOWING OURSELVES TO BE DEFINED AS "MOM" AND "DAD"

When a couple begins to refer to each other as "Mom" and "Dad" even when the kids aren't around, it's the kiss of death for their romance and sex. I firmly believe that a married couple should never lose sight of the fact that they are LOVERS who share a very exclusive and intimate sexual bond. And by making the connection as "Mother" and "Father" to each other instead of husband and wife sets up a psychological, sexual taboo.

The taboos come into play after women give birth because it's common to develop a kind of a role confusion as "Mothers." The psychological image we have of "Mother" is one of a self–sacrificing, non-sexual, ministering person. Let's face it. It's hard for us to EVEN THINK about our mothers having sex with our fathers. It's just something we inherently feel very uncomfortable about. And that same theory applies to ourselves, as well, when we become mothers.

Also, many men have a great deal of difficulty with it. They begin to see their wives as "Mothers" and the old taboos about sex with your mother are reaffirmed. It may sound simplistic but it is very true. It is a common psychological reaction. And so we make it even harder when we contribute to it by defining ourselves as parents first and foremost. In order to keep our marriages and relationships sexual and passionate, we need to maintain that emotional connection to each other as "husbands" and "wives" who support and nurture each other.

So what it all boils down to is an attitude. Do you want to look at each other as "Ma" and "Pa"? Or do you want to define yourselves as LOVERS whose passion and emotional closeness transcends all stereotypes?

5. CHILDREN NEED TO EMOTIONALLY SEPARATE TO BECOME ADULTS

Another reason why marriages have problems establishing and maintaining passion is that either the husband or wife or both, in some cases, did not make the emotional transition from being a son or daughter to a wife or husband. Many people enter a relationship who are still so emotionally bound to their parents that they have a very large problem establishing a good sexual and emotional base in their own marital relationships. They still rely on their parents for the emotional support, unconditional love, and nurturing they should be giving each other as husband and wife.

And this behavior is often transferred to their children when they have them. The parents begin living their lives through and for their kids because of the emotional starvation in their own marriages. And it becomes increasingly hard for them to let go of them emotionally when the kids leave home and get married. And the kids, in turn, will suffer from the same problem when trying to establish their own marital intimacy.

This has been a problem since time began. There is even a passage in the Bible often quoted in wedding ceremonies which talks about a son leaving his parents and "cleaving unto his wife." And it means that an emotional re-attachment from parent to spouse must be made to build a successful marriage. The marital relationship is a unique one. It necessitates total loyalty, love and emotional commitment to ONE PERSON in order to succeed. Don't fall into the trap of allowing anything or anyone else to supersede your emotional commitment with your spouse. To do so is to rob you of the ability to nurture and be nurtured, love and be loved and to give and receive the sexual fulfillment that can only be shared between husband and wife.

What this translates into in practical terms is this:

1. YOUR LOYALTIES HAVE TO BE FIRST AND FOREMOST TO YOUR SPOUSE AFTER MARRIAGE–NOT YOUR PARENTS.

2. YOU NEED TO EXTEND THE SAME UNCONDITIONAL LOVE TO EACH OTHER AS YOU DO TO YOUR CHILDREN.

3. ALLOW YOUR KIDS TO GROW AND MAKE THEIR OWN DECISIONS, WITHIN REASON, WITHOUT CONSTANT INTERFERENCE.

4. YOU ARE RESPONSIBLE FOR RAISING YOUR OWN CHILDREN–IT IS NOT YOUR PARENTS' DOMAIN. SEEKING ADVICE AND SUPPORT IS ONLY NATURAL, BUT YOU MUST MAKE ALL YOUR OWN RULES AND DECISIONS IN THE FINAL ANALYSIS.

5. ALWAYS ENCOURAGE YOUR MARRIED CHILDREN TO SUPPORT AND BE LOYAL FIRST AND FOREMOST TO THEIR SPOUSES AND NOT TO YOU. YOU SHOULD NEVER CREATE SITUATIONS IN WHICH THEIR LOYALTY MUST BE DIVIDED.

6. GIVE YOUR CHILDREN EVERY OPPORTUNITY TO BOND AND BUILD A HEALTHY EMOTIONAL UNION WITH THEIR SPOUSE. GIVE ADVICE WHEN YOU'RE ASKED–OTHERWISE, ALLOW THEM TO GO THROUGH THE NORMAL MATURING PROCESSES ON THEIR OWN. THIS INCLUDES MAKING MISTAKES, JUST LIKE YOU DID!

7. ALWAYS ENCOURAGE THEIR GROWTH AS ADULTS, EVEN IF IT MEANS SACRIFICING SOME OF YOUR OWN PARENTAL DESIRES. FOR EXAMPLE, IF YOUR SON GETS A FABULOUS BUSINESS OPPORTUNITY IN ANOTHER STATE, DON'T DISCOURAGE HIM FROM ACCEPTING IT BECAUSE YOU DON'T WANT HIM TO MOVE AWAY FROM YOU. IT'S PART OF THE PROCESS OF LETTING GO EMOTIONALLY AS A PARENT FOR THE BETTERMENT OF YOUR CHILD.

SUGGESTION BOX

* * * IMPORTANT POINTS TO REMEMBER * * *

1. THE KIND OF LOVE THAT CHILDREN GIVE THEIR PARENTS IS EXTREMELY STRONG AND UNCONDITIONAL IN NATURE. BUT IT SHOULD NEVER REPLACE THE NEED FOR LOVE AND FRIENDSHIP THAT A HUSBAND AND WIFE HAVE FOR EACH OTHER.

2. AFTER THE BABY ARRIVES, YOUR SCHEDULES WILL BE HECTIC. SO YOU WILL NEED TO BE CREATIVE IN RE-ARRANGING AND PLANNING TIME FOR HUSBAND-WIFE NURTURING TO MAINTAIN YOUR OWN EMOTIONAL BONDS.

3. NEVER USE YOUR KIDS AS AN EXCUSE TO IGNORE YOUR OWN NEEDS FOR INTIMACY.

4. KEEP THE BABY OUT OF YOUR BED. MAKE HIS BEDROOM A WARM, PLEASANT AND SAFE ENVIRONMENT FOR HIM TO ENJOY. MOST BABIES CAN BE TRAINED TO HAVE REASONABLE BEDTIME SCHEDULES.

5. POST-PARTUM LACK OF SEXUAL DRIVE IS NORMAL. CONSULT YOUR DOCTOR ON A REGULAR BASIS AND SEEK HIS ADVICE TO HELP EASE YOU THROUGH THIS PERIOD. IT WILL NOT LAST FOREVER!

6. LACK OF SEXUAL DRIVE CAN BE A DIRECT RESULT OF POOR SELF–IMAGE. FOR YOUR PHYSICAL AND MENTAL WELL-BEING, GET YOURSELF ON A REGULAR PROGRAM OF EXERCISE AND SENSIBLE EATING. GETTING BACK INTO SHAPE AFTER THE BABY ARRIVES SHOULD BE A NUMBER ONE PRIORITY FOR YOU.

7. WE ALL LOVE OUR CHILDREN UNCONDITIONALLY, BUT IT'S IMPORTANT TO REMEMBER THAT YOU STILL MUST MAKE AN EFFORT TO HAVE ADULT TIME WITH YOUR SPOUSE. CHILDREN SHOULD NEVER PUT AN END TO MARITAL BONDING OR DAMPEN THE PASSION BETWEEN LOVING PARTNERS.

8. DON'T IDENTIFY YOURSELVES FIRST AND FOREMOST AS "MOM" AND "DAD." MARRIED COUPLES SHOULD NEVER LOSE SIGHT OF THE FACT THAT THEY ARE "LOVERS" WHO SHARE A VERY EXCLUSIVE AND INTIMATE SEXUAL BOND.

9. AFTER MARRIAGE, YOUR LOYALTY AND EMOTIONAL BONDS NEED TO SHIFT FROM YOUR PARENTS TO YOUR SPOUSE. THIS IS A NORMAL COURSE OF EVENTS AND DOES NOT IMPLY ANY FORM OF DISRESPECT TOWARDS YOUR PARENTS.

10. TEACH THIS TO YOUR OWN CHILDREN BY SETTING THE EXAMPLE IN YOUR OWN HOME. IT WILL HELP THEM TO MAKE THEIR OWN TRANSITION INTO FULFILLING RELATIONSHIPS AND MARRIAGE COME NATURALLY WITHOUT FEELING GUILTY THAT THEY ARE DIVIDING THEIR LOYALTY.

CHAPTER 6

SEX AND PASSION

THE ESSENCE OF MARRIAGE

A friend of mine has a therapist who says that if she could get into the bedrooms of all her patients and observe their sexual interaction, she could tell you pretty much how the couples are interacting in all the other facets of their marriage. In other words, the bedroom is the microcosm of the marriage in totality and their sexual interaction is a barometer of how everything else is faring. This struck me as very insightful. Sex is the one act which a husband and wife share between them that no one else in the extended family can be a part of. It's the strongest element in a relationship that will help keep the couple "in love" and passionate about each other throughout their lives.

And when a couple's sex life is non-existent or very sporadic at best, its got to have a profound effect on the passion between them and the rest of their relationship in general. Therefore, couples owe it to each other and to themselves to work on, nurture and improve their sexual interaction.

So why is it that this seems to be so difficult to achieve? Well, in the previous chapters we have talked about how fighting, decreased communication, children and other factors play a very large part in diminishing the couples desire to have sex. We have seen how resentments caused by these factors can build up to a point where the couple will shut down to sex entirely. Now let's explore some of the other things which inhibit women in their sexual practices and talk about methods of overcoming or avoiding these pitfalls. The following are statements made to me by women and men concerning some of the difficulties they have encountered in trying to maintain a passionate sex life.

WHAT MEN WANT WOMEN TO DO

♥♥♥"My husband complains that I never take the role of the 'aggressor' and initiate lovemaking. He says it's a real turn-on to all men and women should do it more often. I suppose he's right, but I just don't feel comfortable doing it. I'm really not sure why."

I am sure this statement comes as no surprise to most women. We hear MANY men voicing this complaint whenever they talk about women. So why aren't we being the aggressors, gals? There are a lot of reasons. But I think the major one stems from how differently men and women learn about sex and form their opinions and values about it at an early age. Men learn about sex on a very visual and physical level. From the time they are blossoming sexually and taking an interest in learning about sex, they look for it in *male-oriented* magazines plus steamy movies and porn films. They talk with other guys or older brothers who present their own versions of "how they got laid"–which can, of course, be highly exaggerated. But that is basically how they learn. There is not the same cultural taboo placed on masturbation for males as it is with females. So boys start at a comparatively young age looking at erotic magazines and masturbate while fantasizing about them. Many times, their first sexual experiences are with the so called "fast" girls or older girls who have prior experience. So it's no wonder that men take a much more earthy and purely physical approach to sex. Furthermore, the women in these films and magazines are presented as highly sexual beings who are aroused by a man's slightest touch or look. Therefore, I think we can all agree that most men in our society learn about sex in a highly biased, unrealistic arena which gives many misconceptions and false ideas about how most women respond to sex.

The second difference in the sexuality of men and women lies in our obvious physical differences. Men have external genitalia which are a lot more sensitive to arousal than a woman's. We have all heard the old adages about how teenage boys continually have a "hard on" from their raging hormones. Well, there happens to be some truth to this. Because of their location and structure, men are much more easily aroused physically than women. Women's genitals are internal and thus, harder to arouse from a physical standpoint. However, there's another element to be taken into consideration. Men, when growing up, don't have the same cultural restrictions about sex placed on them that women do. Men are taught that it's normal or even "cool" to get aroused. Arousal proves their manhood. They are supposed to have sex in their teens as an initiation rite into adulthood. In fact, it is EXPECTED of them. A man who is 21 and still a virgin is often ridiculed or accused of being "gay," but the same behavior in a woman is praised.

Women, on the other hand, learn about sex and their sexual values much differently. Girls grow up reading romance novels where the woman is always "taken" by the man in an atmosphere of satin sheets, candlelight and intense romance. Many women are not as likely to watch porno movies because our culture frowns on it. They will opt instead, to watch equally as unrealistic soap opera sexual encounters or big screen romantic scenes which leave them breathless. We take a much more ethereal and much less earthy approach to sex than men because of how we learn about it. Women are encouraged by their mothers, girlfriends and older sisters not to engage in sex until they are engaged or married. We are constantly warned about the dangers of "giving away sex" too freely and lectured about the moral decay which "cheap sex" leads us into.

And the truth is that very seldom does anybody ever sit down with us and tell us how to actually "have sex." We are always told that it will "come naturally" in the proper environment of love and caring. Well, the sad truth is that most of the time this isn't so. The real facts are that close to 30% of the women I talked to NEVER had an orgasm because nobody told them how to achieve one. They were told that it would just happen spontaneously with enough love from a man. But in reality, this just isn't so.

Keeping this in mind, is it any wonder why women don't initiate sex most of the time with their husbands? Especially women who have bought all the rhetoric about romantic sex. It just doesn't happen for them this way. I believe that if women learned more about sex the way that men did and vice-versa, the two sexes would come to a better understanding of how the other thinks about it. If men were taught and truly understood the NEED FOR ROMANCE that women attach to sex, and if women learned to be a little bit more uninhibited and basic about sex, we would all do a lot better!! The good news is that I have observed this happening more frequently with the present younger generation but the bad news is that the older generation missed out on it. However, don't despair, gals. Regardless of what generation you belong to, I'm going to give you some real answers to your problems. Read on.

HOW TO GET "SEXIER"

1. PSYCHOLOGICALLY RE-ADJUST YOUR EXPECTATIONS:

First, you'll need to work on getting rid of those pre-determined fantasies about the white canopied bed and Prince Charming sweeping you away. If you don't, you are always going to be disappointed in your sexual encounters with your spouse, because he'll NEVER live up to the fantasy you have created in your head. Instead, get into the habit of approaching sex more like a man, psychologically speaking. Think about the sensations and the pleasure you're going to feel instead of just expecting a plethora of romantic words. Dress like the aggressor. This means ditching those flannel night gowns with the lace around the neck and putting on a sexy nightie! Dress to impress! You will be amazed at how much more sexy and aggressive you're going to feel. Don't put any expectations on your spouse. Just enjoy the sex for the sheer pleasure of it. Remember, expectations invariably bring about disappointments.

Also, don't keep putting off making love until the "right moment." A lot of women can't psychologically get into sex unless everything in their environment feels right–the laundry is done, there are no immediate problems standing between you, or you have just showered, etc.–things of this nature. But let's be realistic. There's NEVER going to be "a perfect time." There will always be something which makes it "less than perfect." So stop searching for perfection and get into the habit of *seizing the moment!*

2. LEARN MORE ABOUT THE PHYSIOLOGY OF SEX ITSELF:

Many women aren't really into sex because they have trouble achieving orgasm. They rationalize this problem by saying that "it's no big deal to have an orgasm" and they enjoy just being "held and cuddled." Well, you know something? You're never going to like sex and become the aggressor if all you settle for is some cuddling. You are MISSING THE BOAT ladies! If you are non-orgasmic there are several great books out on the market about how to become orgasmic. Just go to the "self-help" or "human sexuality" section of your bookstore and choose a few. Two of my favorite books which are highly informative are "For Yourself" and "For Each Other" by Lonnie Barbach, Ph.D. But, whatever you choose, you must read them and DO WHAT THEY TELL YOU. Many involve learning how to masturbate or practicing other physical techniques which will help get your sexual responses going. Now, I know that a lot of women may find this distasteful at first. However, you have got to keep the big picture in mind. And that is: You want to become a much more sexually responsive woman. You want to experience orgasm and learn to really enjoy sex and your own sexuality. And to do this, *you're going to HAVE TO shed some of those old inhibitions* which have been preventing you from achieving it in the first place.

It will make it easier if you begin to examine your attitudes on sex in the context of how you were raised. You may have been told that sex was "dirty" or sex was only to "please a man." Or you may have listened to sermons in church which denounced sex and sexual women. When we go back and examine some of that old input, we will begin to realize that the old taboos and negative thoughts about sexuality are just plain stupid. When you really examine them closely, they make very little sense. I am not suggesting that we can shed these attitudes which have been indoctrinated into us over the years in a matter of days or weeks. But make it a practice to use more critical thinking while you're re-educating yourself with current information. Then it will become possible to re-adjust your attitudes in many areas. Always remember, you are married and making love is a beautiful experience.

If you feel that the books or manuals you have read aren't helping you sufficiently, you might seek counseling to make your transition easier. But you must adopt the priority: You want to become a sensual and sexual woman. You want to develop a strong desire to really enjoy sex with your husband and not just *succumb* to it anymore. You want to feel and enjoy sex as much as he does. And if these are the goals you truly want to achieve, then re–educating yourself through books, manuals, tapes, seminars or counseling will help you get there. And, when you begin to feel a real change in your attitudes and perceptions from your new sexual awareness, your husband is going to sit up and take notice. Believe me, you will turn him on incredibly with your new attitude. And in the process, you will be delighted to find that you are turning yourself on too! Your new attitude will free you psychologically to become the aggressor as often as you want in your relationship.

"ONE-WAY" SEX

♥♥"My wife used to be a lot more uninhibited about sex during our courtship. We had frequent oral sex, experimented with a lot of different positions and she spent a good deal of time massaging and caressing my sensitive areas. But now our sex is always limited to a straight missionary position because she doesn't want to do it any other way. It makes me wonder whether she cares less for me now or was she just putting on a 'big show' to win me into marriage? I know I'm not the only guy with this problem, because many of my friends complain about the same thing."

This is a situation that we hear men complain about very frequently. We have already heard in a previous chapter from a woman who admitted to this behavior. Is it because women really do *audition* for their men before they get married? Do they engage in a variety of sexual behaviors they don't really like just to *lure* them into marriage? Or, if they really did enjoy it before marriage what makes them change their attitudes after marriage?

I believe that both situations are true. There are many women who feel that they HAVE TO perform a lot of sexual acts to keep a man interested. They want to make men believe that they are *very sexual* human beings. They do it, obviously, because they believe this is what a man wants and expects from a woman. However, the fallacy in this behavior is that they haven't thought it through to the consequences. What's going to happen to their relationships once they stop acting *very sexual?* They may figure that the man will just have to get used to it, because after they're married he won't have much of a choice. But, of course, this is a big mistake because the marriage license is only the beginning of a lifetime of interaction. The relationship has got to grow and be nurtured sexually and emotionally on a continual basis. And denying sex acts that were once a part of their relationship isn't going to fly with the man. It's going to put a big wall of resentment and rejection between them.

THE SECOND EXPLANATION

From the women I've talked to and the research I've done, I have discovered something else to be true. Most women actually did enjoy the sexual experimentation with their mates, but it was other factors after marriage which worked in a negative way to dampen their desires. Look at it this way. The straight missionary position during sex is one that requires the least amount of submission and intimacy. I believe that it is the extreme intimacy of the other sexual acts which prevents a woman from engaging in them freely. By nature, they demand complete communication, lack of resentment and a total environment of unconditional love. And these elements are what is lacking in so many of these marriages thus putting an end to these sexual practices.

And, in the normal course of marital discords, crises and arguments, when a woman finds herself blanketed in resentment and with bad feelings towards her spouse the LAST thing she wants to do is perform an act that by it's very nature is submissive. This would apply to oral sex, anal sex or sex in different positions where the man is dominant. It's also the same old case of the less you do it the less you desire it. Making love by utilizing the practices of oral sex or alternative positions takes more time and is a lot more physical. When a woman gets out of practice, the thought of what's involved in these acts makes them a lot less desirable to perform.

This is not to say that I am endorsing these acts of lovemaking as musts in any relationship. As with anything else in a conjugal relationship, it is strictly up to the desire of both parties. What I AM saying, however, is that if these acts were once included in your lovemaking menu, to deny them completely at any point in the marriage can't help but be taken as a form of rejection by your spouse.

HOW TO GET BACK INTO IT

1. First you've got to recall in detail those old days of lovemaking when you had an *anything goes* attitude and enjoyed everything you did. Try to

remember the sensations and erotic feelings these acts brought out in you. If your inhibitions are keeping you from performing certain sexual acts now, then it's important to recall how uninhibited and shameless you felt then. And to help you overcome your inhibitions, try reading some steamy novels or watching some soft-core erotic films. This is adopting the same "visual" methods of getting aroused as men do. And it's highly effective for them, as we well know. And when you see other women enjoying the same acts without shame, it's going to help *free you up* to become a more willing participant. It may take a few months or so to knock down those walls of inhibition and develop the attitude that these acts are expressions of deep love and not something "dirty."

2. Clear the air between you and your husband emotionally. If there is some lingering resentment towards him standing in your way, it's got to be resolved. Remember, you are attempting to put something very vital back into your marriage. And it's going to take forgiveness and solid communication to get there. If the problems between you are of a deep-rooted and long-standing nature, then get help from a counselor or other source in resolving them. It's only natural that you are not going to perform oral sex on him if you feel like you'd rather be biting it off now. It may sound funny, but it's absolutely true for women. There are sexual acts that demand such an intimate part of ourselves, women won't do them unless it's in an environment of total love without any traces of ill-feelings towards the man.

3. Spend time getting SENSUAL before you get SEXUAL. Lie in bed together, stroking, exploring, kissing and caressing his body parts. Let him do the same to you. Do this for a week or so WITHOUT worrying about it ending up in intercourse. Take a bubble bath together, massage each other with fragrant oil, light aromatic candles and play romantic music. In other words, surround yourself with an aura of soothing beauty and tenderness. This will help you get in touch with feelings that have been dormant for a long time. You will begin to relax and let the resentment out and the love back in. Again, this doesn't happen in mere minutes or even days. It takes a long time to peel away those layers of bad feelings. But keep in mind that IT CAN BE DONE. I guarantee that once the resentment melts away and is replaced by some of those old loving sensations, it will be quite natural for you to progress from stroking to giving oral sex or whatever urge you feel.

Now I know what a lot of women will respond with when they read this. I've heard all the protests before. Things like: "My husband would never go for simply petting" or "it's unrealistic to fill the room with flowers and candles every time." Well, let me respond to both. First of all, if you explain to your husband that this is a method you are using to restore your sexual urges and help make you more responsive in lovemaking, he'd be an IDIOT to say no! Come on ladies! Did you ever hear ONE MAN on EARTH protest to getting oral sex?? He'll love it. And *he will go along with whatever it takes to get you going again.* And secondly, the candles and all the rest of the paraphernalia are very important in staging the scene which brings about your relaxation and ultimate arousal. If you had an illness that required some time consuming cure, you wouldn't just say "forget it–it takes too much time!" Of course not. But this is just as important. We're talking about curing you emotionally and getting rid of your inhibitions. It's all a necessary part to effect the change and restore the original passion you felt for each other. Ladies, what can be more important than that!

4. Start thinking of yourself as a woman who has a definite sexual persona instead of a little girl trying to please. Keep in mind that you also have the right to receive as much pleasure as you give. Both sexes help each other towards orgasm but ultimately, the orgasm comes from within your own body. YOU ARE RESPONSIBLE for it. When you make this shift in thinking, it will be of an immense help to emotionally loosen you up sexually. *Keep thinking of yourself as an ADULT woman who has sexual needs*–the same as any other woman. And stop thinking of yourself as the person in the relationship who has the duty to please her man. This thinking is self-defeating and archaic. You have the same RIGHT to be sexually fulfilled as your spouse does. You need to please each other!

5. Dress the part for a sensual encounter. I've said it before. Get rid of those flannel nighties and granny-styled bed clothes. If you dress *sexy*, you're going to feel a lot more sexual. And those silky teddies have a wonderful side effect–your husband will get really turned on by just looking at you wearing one. But more importantly, they *will* get you in the mood. But DO IT FOR YOURSELF and you'll automatically be doing it for him, too. You'll be delighted in the difference it makes for both of you!

HOW MANY TIMES IS NORMAL?

♥♥"My wife thinks that making love once a week is perfectly normal. But I feel horny and rejected all the time. You bet I don't think it's enough. Every night is my idea of enough."

Let me state first of all that the FREQUENCY of sex doesn't insure a great marriage. Couples who have sex five times a week are not necessarily happier than couples who do it once a week. Don't make the mistake of looking for any magic number by which to evaluate your love life. The truth is that a husband and wife should be comfortable with a pattern they BOTH AGREE ON. It's only when you are miles apart like this woman's one night vs. her husband's seven nights, that you'll need to work toward a compromise. However, if you are having sex once a week and THOROUGHLY ENJOYING it, then the question becomes why aren't you doing it more often?

Sexual excitement is a thing that feeds on itself. As I've stated before, the more you do it, the more you want to do it. And when you really think about it ladies, are there many things that feel better than an orgasm? I think one of the basic problems is that we all get LAZY. In our hectic lives, there isn't a long stretch of time when we don't feel overwhelmed or tired. This is normal. But we can't let it begin to erode our marriages, because there's no point in that. Knocking yourself out to create the perfect home only to have the people who live in it fall apart after a few years is self-defeating in every sense of the word. We can't sexually starve ourselves because it will emotionally kill our marriages.

There are happily married women who have sex ranging from every day of the week down to once a week or less. What works for them is what they AGREE on with their husbands. And remember, nothing is written in stone. There will be times when it's impossible to have sex at all during one week and other times when you'll have it every day. In relationships, things have a way of evening out over time.

There are also a lot of women who have learned to repress so many of their feelings that it has left them emotionally and physically *numb* when it comes to sex. However, these are women who appear perfectly serene and content on the outside because they have learned to stuff all their feelings and put a smile on their faces for the outside world. But in doing this, they suppress ALL their emotions and not just the bad ones. They have no highs or lows. Everything has been emotionally tucked away to a point where they don't deal with it anymore. And the real danger is that these women become ANESTHETIZED to life.

It becomes most apparent in the sexual arena, because they have no desire for sex and never enjoy it when they do. So they put it off day after day with one excuse or another, while maintaining that outward facade of everything being just fine. But of course it isn't. Their lack of feeling will surely be taken as a rejection by their husbands and arouse their anger, hurt and resentment. Then they will be obliged to stuff the problems arising from his feelings too. So you can see how repression builds a most dangerous cycle in a relationship. Repressed people will need counseling to help them deal with their problems and to learn how to open themselves up again to the hurts as well as the pleasures. It's a must in order to keep those people emotionally and spiritually alive.

HOW TO STOP "PUTTING OFF" SEX

1. Don't wait for the perfect moment to have sex and then keep putting it off when it doesn't materialize. You must come to the full realization that you're going to ruin your marriage if you do this over time. So even if you're tired, make the effort and do it. And guess what? There will come a point when you're getting really turned on and enjoying your body's responses so much, you'll forget you were tired! Pretty miraculous, huh? I am not saying that this will be the case EVERY time, but you'll be surprised how much of the time it happens. This is because sex actually happens in our heads. When you *give permission* to yourself to become truly committed to making love, it will supersede your physical feelings of exhaustion. This is because many times you aren't really *tired*, you are just not in the mood for other reasons.

2. Be flexible in your scheduling of sex. Don't get into the routine of having it only at night when you go to bed. It's often the worst time for most of us, because we are wiped out by 11 or 12 at night. Try making love in the morning. Upon awakening, the sleepy and relaxed state of your body is actually a big help in allowing sexual feelings to arise. I think you'll find that you can be aroused a lot more quickly in the morning when you are relaxed and your mind is clear after a good night's sleep. Your brain is where it's happening anyway. And, after a long day, it's cluttered with thoughts of the day, what you need to do tomorrow and all kinds of other demands. You're not focused. But in the morning, it's like waking up with a clean slate. So, when possible, take advantage of those serene morning hours.

3. Remember to KISS. Therapists will tell you that many people who have been married a long time rarely kiss at all. They go straight into intercourse. But this is like eating the cone and throwing away the ice cream. Kissing will help establish closeness and allow your sexual feelings to flow much more readily. Remember when you were in high school and you just *made out* for hours–and loved it? Reestablish your practice of holding each other and kissing each other passionately. It will help turn you back on to sex and you'll find that once a week isn't enough for you anymore.

THE ROLE OF FANTASY

♥♥"I would really love to get my wife into more fantasy and role-playing during sex. I see it in movies and it's such a turn on! We used to do a little of it but now she thinks it's ridiculous and won't do it anymore."

As with anything that's a departure from your norm, it all lies in the perception of things. A lot of women might see this fantasy or role playing thing as *kinky* so they rule it out without giving it another thought. But let me tell you something which might surprise you. *The women who told me they did engage in fantasy during sex said it changed their sex lives and sexual attitudes 360 degrees–for the better.*

These were women who said that before doing it, they never felt "sexual" and used to feel inhibited about having sex. They felt like they were working hard at something they really didn't want to do anyway. Some said it was because they had bad self–images of their bodies. Others said they just couldn't see THEMSELVES as sex kittens. But when they put on a French Maid's costume or played the role of a hooker seducing their husbands–WOW –things changed. One woman explained it this way:

"I became the persona of 'Monique the French Maid' and began seducing my husband. I couldn't believe how much I GOT INTO IT! And do you know why? Because it was 'Monique' doing those things and not me. Psychologically, 'Monique' was free to act out any fantasy she wanted to and I didn't feel embarrassed because SHE was doing all these things–not me. So when 'Monique' performed oral sex on my husband and he got excited, she got turned on even more. For some reason, I would not allow that to happen when it was ME, but it was okay when I became someone else."

This woman was so excited about her newfound sexual revelations that it made me want to run out and buy a costume that very minute!! But then I remembered that I already had one! When you think about it–it makes a lot of sense. Women who have, for whatever reasons, branded themselves as "unsexy" and "unappealing" really believe it to be true. They have internalized it to the degree that it has sexually inhibited them so severely, the thought of themselves having sex seemed *ludicrous*. But when they take on an alter-ego supplied by a costume or a fantasy, it allows them to by–pass that old image of themselves, and hence, their inhibitions. And it works! Countless women have told me it does.

Now is this a *healthy* thing to do? Why not? You are helping yourself get past a huge stumbling block and therefore your partner benefits too. You are both reaping enormous benefits. This, in itself, makes it *healthy*. Does this mean you'll have to be "Heidi" or "Colette" for the rest of your life to enjoy sex? Not necessarily. I think that after you get into the whole enjoyable process of feeling, responding and becoming orgasmic, you'll get to the point where you won't need the costume. Maybe you'll progress to role playing and then to a diet mixed with equal parts of fantasy and non-fantasy as your *normal* sexual scenario. It's like training wheels on a bike. After you get your confidence and skills honed, you'll take off without them. And if you never *take them off*–so what? You're feeling, enjoying and having a great time– something you weren't able to do before. And there's nothing bad about that?

We'll discuss this more in the section about "tips that will make your sex life sizzle." In this chapter you'll read an actual letter I got from a woman who employed a fantasy and had the best sexual experience of her life. There's nothing like real-life testimony to help open up your eyes and your mind to new experiences.

WHAT WOMEN WANT THEIR MEN TO DO FOR THEM

♥♥"Are all the men out there like my husband? Did they all forget what the word f-o-r-e-p-l-a-y means after they got married? It's like he goes right for the genitals without even so much as a caress or kiss to warm me up. It's no small wonder to me that many men complain they 'never get it' from their wives."

There are countless women who have voiced the same complaint. Most women absolutely hate it when a man goes straight for their genitals. It feels INVASIVE to them. Women positively need to feel that closeness and tenderness before they can warm up to the actual act of penetration. Our bodies and psyches demand it. And only then, the act of intercourse will confirm that intimacy. But it rarely creates it on it's own with nothing else.

And even though it is a woman's right to receive the foreplay to create the intimacy, unfortunately, men aren't mind readers. So *if they aren't doing this for you, then you'll have to TELL THEM WHAT YOU WANT.* You can set the stage with music and candles if you wish, but first set aside some time to have a little chat with your husband. Explain that you would be much more willing to have sex more frequently, if only he would take the time to provide you with more loving foreplay. And then spell it out for him. Be specific about how and where you want to be caressed, kissed, stimulated orally or whatever your personal desires encompass. If you explain it to him beforehand, then you'll avoid getting put in the position of being the *director* in bed. And, if he isn't extending the foreplay long enough for you to become fully aroused, let him know it. Whisper some erotic stuff in his ear which will give him the incentive to carry on with what he's doing. The proof will be in the pudding so to speak, when he sees how aroused you're becoming and how much more willing you are to give back to him. Also remember, your giving him foreplay will be an additional stimulant.

And while were on the subject of foreplay, let's not forget the afterplay too. Women hate it when men roll over and go to sleep after they've had their orgasm. It's like wrapping the present and forgetting the big bow on top. *We don't want to feel like our bodies have been used and then summarily dismissed.* We want to be cuddled and bask in the after-glow for awhile. Explain this to him. Tell him that you realize that most men don't expect or feel the need for excessive cuddling and romancing but women do. Women must have the whole ball of wax–the kissing, massaging, stroking and the tender words to bring them to their fullest response. And when we're getting all of this, it will stimulate our desire to want sex a lot more often than we did without it.

HOW TO MAKE HIM INTO A "FOREPLAY WIZARD"

1. Tell him what you want beforehand. Then, when he is trying to please you, really encourage him!! You can do it verbally by telling him how wonderful he's making you feel and how turned on you're getting. Praise his efforts. And then return them. Stroke his back, kiss him passionately and caress him. Do to him what he's doing to you. Add some erotic whispers and tenderness too. Put the same creative energy into your lovemaking as you would into the things you love to do the most. Give it the importance it deserves in the context of your marriage and your lives together.

2. During the course of foreplay or the sex act itself, don't GIVE ORDERS! Refrain from constantly giving directions like, "a little more over here" or "not so hard on my thigh" or ""put your hand here." Instead, do it by placing his hands where it feels good and turning your body in positions that please you. Men do not want to feel like they are being taught. It will crush that fragile male ego. Use your cleverness and womanly savvy to make him do what feels good for you. A moan of encouragement is all he'll need to keep him going in the right direction!

3. Begin the foreplay long before you hit the sheets! Kiss him while he's shaving in the bathroom or caress him before you go up to bed. Touch him frequently all evening while you're watching TV. In essence, use that interaction of closeness as the momentum to be carried on after you go to bed. A little of this will go a long way to get you both into a loving and giving frame of mind.

STRESS AND SEX

♥♥"I feel that the stress level of my husband's job and my daily responsibilities of home and family are constantly getting in the way of our ability to have really fulfilling sex. He's usually exhausted, preoccupied or in the middle of some crisis that keeps his thoughts from being totally focused on us when we're making love. This goes for me too. I blame the pressures of today's busy lifestyles on our dwindling sexual desires."

Stress seems to be a product of the hectic, technological age we live in. And it happens to be a very real phenomenon. I think we've all read the articles about *yuppie burnout* and how it adversely affects people's sex lives. Young couples obsess so much about their jobs and *getting ahead* that it literally saps all their energy, leaving almost nothing for sexual passion. So why are we devoting so much of ourselves to our careers yet allowing our relationships to starve? Well, it's a question of priority. It's easy to allow our careers to become the priority instead of the marriage. We keep telling ourselves that when we can afford the big house, or have the money to travel, or make enough to hire the nanny, THEN we can devote ourselves to each other more fully. But, you know what? That day may NEVER COME. It's just the nature of who we are. As I've stated before: continually postponing our sexual and emotional needs will eventually KILL THE RELATIONSHIP. We may get fat with our money and possessions, but emotionally, we will starve. And until we can really grasp that message and accept it, our relationships are going to remain in ever-increasing peril.

There is an all too common scenario in which highly successful couples, after finally moving into their *dream house*, split up. Everyone around them is shocked. But when you think about it, it isn't so surprising at all. They have sacrificed their relationship in the ultimate attainment of the material goals which they thought would bring them closer. But what they find is that they're living in this big, beautiful home with no love and no bonds left between them. The disillusionment is just too much to bear and they separate physically. But the emotional separation started when they sacrificed nurturing each other in their goal to attain the very thing they thought would bring them together. Ironic isn't it? But sadly, this happens far too often in today's materialistic oriented society.

AVOIDING THAT TRAP

1. *You have got to put your marriage and the nurturing of each other ABOVE everything else.* And to do this, you have to accept this concept: MATERIAL GAINS WILL NEVER TAKE THE PLACE OF THE EMOTIONAL NURTURING YOU MUST PROVIDE FOR ONE ANOTHER ON A DAILY BASIS. If it means cutting back on your work and sacrificing the raise or whatever, so be it. You have to keep the sanctity of your marriage as the number one priority in your lives. Without that, what do you really have?

2. Take as many vacations alone with each other as possible. If you can't afford to jump on a plane, then go to a nearby hotel on one of their superspecial "price buster" weekends. Most men and women find the atmos-

phere of a hotel room very conducive to romance and lovemaking. It's very important to just remove yourself physically from all the stress-causing factors around you. It's too easy to accept business calls at home on the weekends and succumb to the same old pressures when you're career-oriented. So become LOVE-ORIENTED for that special weekend and carry those good feelings from your heart right into your home. Practice this until they are so deeply ingrained that they will take precedence over everything else that robs your attention from each other.

3. Permit yourselves two free hours every evening when neither of you discusses your jobs, the kids' problems or any other stressful matters. Schedule your time for relaxation TOGETHER and indulge in a relaxing jacuzzi or give each other massages. Make it a priority to include lots of stress reducing activities which are also conducive to romance and good communication. Remember, relaxation is the best avenue to great sex. You OWE it to yourselves and to your relationship.

4. Learn how to have FUN together all over again. Recall the kinds of activities you did when dating and try them again. Roller–blading, dancing, walks in the park or on the beach or any type of uplifting physical activities you can do together are wonderful ways to re-bond. *Make an effort to make each other laugh again.* Remember when it was SOOO important to be witty and fun? It's so easy to forget how we did it. And don't forget to let that humor and fun carry over into the bedroom as well. Have fun with sex! Laugh at the silly things that happen in the course of lovemaking. Make it a priority to lighten up and start enjoying your lives together.

WORDS OF LOVE

♥♥"What I want from my husband is more communication during lovemaking. It's been ages since he's expressed tenderness verbally. He rarely tells me he loves me anymore or that I'm sexy or how beautiful I look to him. It's something I definitely need to hear in order to get the romantic juices flowing. I find it extremely hard to work up any passion with a man who expresses so little."

This is a problem that has been expressed by most women to varying degrees. The difference lies in the fact that men are sexually very VISUAL creatures, while women are more verbal. Sex happens for women in their heads BEFORE it happens in their bodies. Men can just LOOK at erotic movies or pictures and get turned on. Put a mirror on the ceiling and they're in heaven! But it doesn't happen for women in this way. We need to HEAR how much we are loved. We need the affirmation and approval from our spouses that we are sexy and appreciated BEFORE we can get turned on. The environment of intimacy has got to be set BEFORE the sex act occurs. Sex doesn't necessarily CREATE intimacy, whereas *intimacy is vital in creating sex for women.*

Where our attitudes come from is fairly easy to see. We were brought up to respect ourselves and our female bodies. We were told that we should never allow ourselves to be used FOR A MAN'S SHEER PLEASURE. Love had to be a main ingredient. We were told that it was imperative that we had a man's respect and we should never give ourselves away unless all the other elements were present. And when we make love with our husbands, those beliefs are still with us. We need to be shown and told how much we are loved and adored. And when we don't hear it, our minds instinctively shut down our sexual responsiveness.

This is something men NEED TO GET. It would make their lives so much less complicated if they really understood how deeply this is ingrained in women. So, as with any other situation, if he doesn't know this, you'll have to clue him in. Explain how and why this is so important to you. And then show him how much more responsive you'll be to him when he takes the time to communicate what you need to hear from him.

HOW TO GET HIM TO TALK–IN BED AND OUT OF BED

1. The best way to teach anybody anything is by example. So take it upon yourself to get the dialogue going. Tell him how precious he is to you and how much you appreciate everything he does for you and the family. Tell him how you love his smell, the nape of his neck or the muscles in his legs. Believe it or not, *men need their strokes as much as women do.* Nudge him a little to get him started during foreplay. Whisper little affirmations which will keep him doing what you like. When he's stroking your body, ask him to tell you what he likes most about it. Or just say, "tell me how much you love me." It won't take long to get a dialogue going when he sees how responsive you're becoming.

2. Make it a practice of continuing some of that bedtime dialogue throughout the day. A little praise and admiration here and there will do wonders for your communication with him. It's human nature to return kindness when it's given to someone. Make it a practice to do this often until it becomes second nature to both of you. Men often avoid discussions when they think it's going to lead to criticism of them or be about something they didn't do. Make an effort to always balance out the negatives with positives. Both of you will get a tremendous boost in the self-esteem department. And a good sense of self-esteem is one of the main ingredients in maintaining a good emotional and physical love-life.

3. Remember when you used to talk about your hopes and dreams, your likes and dislikes or what you did during the day that made you happy? You spent a lot of time discussing what you could do together that would make both of you happy. This is the kind of soul-mate type conversations we had in the past that helped bond our relationships like glue. In today's jargon we call it *having good vibes* between people. And what I keep hearing from these married women is that, in essence, they don't have those good vibes anymore. I believe it's because they have stopped having the kind of soul-mate communication where they discuss what they need emotionally from each other and not just problems or mundane daily matters. Your interest in each other's thoughts as people shouldn't stop just because you got married. You are still two growing, evolving, individuals who need to keep re-bonding and re-nurturing yourselves over and over again. Sharing your inner thoughts and dreams opens you up to your loved ones and substitutes resentment and indifference with real caring and love. When you know that you LOVE and TRUST that other person more than anybody else in this world, it is a feeling that transcends everything else. It is spiritual. And when this is added into the mix of lovemaking, you will have some of the most fulfilling and wonderful sexual bonding that can ever be accomplished between a man and a woman.

TIPS FOR KEEPING THE SIZZLE

1. GO DANCING – After marriage many couples lose that PHYSICAL bonding they had when dating. In time, they stop holding hands, hugging and just touching one another on a daily basis. A great way to re-establish some of that physicality AND have fun at the same time is to dance together. There's nothing like the feeling of being held and having your bodies move synchronously to music. It's sexy, romantic and will do wonders to restore your physical closeness. Or, if you had another activity you both loved early in the relationship, try doing that again.

2. LIGHTEN UP – Work on putting some humor back into your relationship. It's a great tension cutter and a very effective way of keeping you connected. Sharing a good laugh together will allow you to feel really "in touch" with one another. And don't forget to have fun in the bedroom too. Taking ourselves less seriously will automatically take a lot of stress off the relationship. Too many people view marriage as a forgone conclusion that the fun in life has to stop. It should be just the opposite. You have the love and security you have always been looking for, so now it should be a lot easier to enjoy each other and your life together.

3. FOCUS ON BEING SENSUAL – When you are heightened to your own SENSUALITY, your SEXUALITY will automatically happen. Wear those delicious silk nighties to bed. Sleep on satin sheets. Wear perfume to bed and dab a little on the sheets. Take hot baths together. Light up your bedroom with a beautiful peach-colored nite-light. Turn the radio on to some easy listening music. Give each other massages. Create that aura of sensuality and bask in it. Allow your body to soak in and delight in the sounds, smells and touching that will bring out your sensual side. And make sure you allow plenty of time to really experience it to the fullest. The state of being highly aroused doesn't happen for women in 5 or 10 minutes. There's no set rule. Just relax, and take whatever time you need to become fully aroused by the sensuality. Remember that rushed sex is unfulfilling sex. You have both earned this time together, so take your time and enjoy every second of it!

4. KEEP YOUR EYES OPEN SOME OF THE TIME – I've noticed that a lot of married couples never really LOOK at one another in the normal course of interaction. So, I can only assume that during lovemaking, they never open their eyes. Don't shut your partner out of your space by doing this. When you are kissing, whispering endearments or caressing each other, LOOK at what you are doing sometimes. It can be such a turn-on. Enjoy watching him get aroused. Exchange those loving glances that only the eyes can convey. Don't be like the little kid on the roller coaster who presses his eyes shut tightly and then opens them when it's over. This is denying the reality of what's happening. Keeping your eyes open and observing what's going on between you during sex is the mark of a woman who has really accepted her own sexuality.

5. PROTECTING THE MALE EGO – Remember the discussion about HOW and WHERE men learn about sex? It's on another planet as far as women are concerned. Couple this with the fact that he's not a mind reader so you've got your work cut out for you. You'll need to explain why foreplay is so important to you– BEFORE the act of intercourse happens. But keep in mind that most men have very fragile egos where their sexuality is concerned. Therefore, be gentle and non-threatening in your approach. Explain it by saying that you're not criticizing what he has been doing, but you do feel he should know more about your needs in order for you to RESPOND AS FULLY as he would like you to. Be aware that any form of condescension is going to make the whole thing backfire. So compromise is a must here. You'll get much better results from him if you come from a non-judgmental position. Remember, a good approach will get good results. And a good result is what you're after–for both of you.

6. WORK ON OVERCOMING YOUR SEXUAL INHIBITIONS – We have talked about the importance of role playing and fantasy in the bedroom. Utilize it. Read up on human sexuality. You are never too old to learn about your own body or the techniques which make it more sexually responsive. Attack this project with the same zeal you would in preparing for a speech or putting on a fabulous dinner party. Nobody sat down and demonstrated the methods of having great sex for any of us. It was always inferred that great sex will come *naturally*. Well, it doesn't. It would shock most men to learn how many of their wives never experienced an orgasm. I've heard it so many times that it doesn't surprise me anymore. But what does surprise me is the *reluctance of women to take responsibility for having their own orgasms*. The truth is that a man doesn't GIVE YOU ONE. You are ultimately responsible for that. He can lead you up to one, but achieving it is your own responsibility.

So, if you have been non-orgasmic in the past, make it a priority to become orgasmic. Stop thinking that you are just one of those women who are "non-orgasmic by nature." Every woman on earth has the ability to have one!! But to learn how, you'll have to practice what the manuals tell you. You may find it uncomfortable at first, but the end results will change your entire consciousness about the importance of sex in your marriage. Get out of your denial about believing that you don't need to have an orgasm to really enjoy sex. Would a man settle for just being cuddled like a woman would? Of course he wouldn't. So why should you?

7. TAKE VACATIONS – Alone time together is essential in keeping you emotionally and physically connected. It's impossible to remove all the stress of day-to-day living. So take frequent breaks from it. But do it together without anyone else along. Too many couples feel that in order to have any "fun" on a vacation they have to take an entourage of friends or family with them. Stop putting other people or your kids between you. This does nothing to help re-establish your closeness. When you are in love and truly in sync with each other, you'll want to be alone as much as possible because you truly enjoy each other's company. Don't let this slip away in your relationship. At first, you may feel ill at ease and find you don't have much to say to each other. This is because you have lost so much of your bonding. However, being alone in the beginning will force you to deal directly with one another. And after a while, you'll have re-established enough of your old closeness to look forward to more alone time together.

8. TRY MARRIAGE ENCOUNTER OR OTHER SIMILAR PROGRAMS – If you have come to the realization that your relationship needs *heavy-duty* repair, then by all means seek the help you need. I have heard rave

reviews from couples who attended "marriage encounter weekends." They claim it did more positive things for their relationship in a few days than they could ever have done by themselves in a year. The seminars combined with the fervent desire to work at re-establishing closeness can be one of the most powerful remedial tools available to couples in need.

9. RECALL PAST HOT SEXUAL TIMES TOGETHER – When a couple recalls some of their hottest and most loving moments together– like certain vacations or loving weekends or hot nights together, the mental images can stir up some of the lost feelings. Re-live them in your heads. You will be surprised at the things you will recall–like his touch or the smell of the cologne he wore, or the way in which you surprised yourself by becoming such a sexual animal! It's simply human nature to forget these times no matter how positive they were. But, recalling them together should be used as a tool whenever possible. Then use the images to create future memorable times together. Remember, you must be responsible for constantly CREATING your romance and your sexual bonding.

10. WOMEN SHOULD TRY TO THINK MORE LIKE MEN IN THEIR APPROACH TO SEX – This statement may be easily misunderstand, so I'll explain it in detail. I have found in talking to women that many of them tend to set up TOO many unrealistic expectations about sex itself. I am not saying that tenderness, caring, love, romance and all the other ingredients aren't necessary. But over the course of your married life, it is self-defeating to expect every single one of them all the time during sex. Men approach sex much more basically and seem to be able to enjoy sex just for the sheer physicality of the act. I think women need to be able to do this MORE OFTEN.

Stop waiting for everything to be perfect in order to make love. It will rarely happen this way. There are many times when we can set the stage with candles and music, but there's also nothing wrong with a delightful *quickie* where we have NO EXPECTATIONS in mind but a great orgasm. You already know that the love is always there between you. I believe that it is entirely possible for women to adopt a more physical attitude through sexually educating their bodies in the ways we've talked about before. When we take the time to teach our bodies how to become orgasmic, it will be a lot easier to assume a more male-like approach to sex. Believe me, when this happens, you are going to overcome a lot of the disappointments in your sex life generated by unfulfilled expectations.

11. BE EACH OTHERS CHEERLEADERS THROUGHOUT LIFE –
Respecting each other and being proud of each other is absolutely essential
to nurturing your relationship. We all have flaws and it's easy to find them.
However, it is most important to dwell on the positives of each other's per-
sonalities and keep these foremost in your minds at all times. Praise each
other and let each other know how much you appreciate each other. It
works miracles. The kind of thinking that makes you afraid he may get
"too big for his britches," if you praise him too often, is just plain stupid.
In fact, it works to the contrary. The more you contribute to building your
partner's self-esteem, the better your relationship will be.

It's most important to be tuned into each other and be able to read each
other's body language to recognize when your partner is depressed, afraid
or whatever it is he's feeling. This is being sensitive to another's feelings.
And the more respect you give one another, the stronger your love will
become throughout your marriage. Remember, you are both growing and
evolving people. And likewise, your marriage is a growing and evolving
entity. Who else better than your spouse to get your positive strokes from?
This old adage is so true: The more you give the more you get. And it
applies to your relationship a hundred times over.

CHAPTER 7

TRUST

TWO WORDS THAT KEEP POPPING UP

During the course of writing this book, I was invited to a number of dinner parties around the country with dozens of women who wanted to have a discussion about many topics relevant to some of the chapters. I love these *female bonding* nights. Surrounded by friendly intelligent women, a great dinner, and a few glasses of wine, it's the perfect setting for women to open up and tell me how they really feel about many issues involving relationships. We had a great cross-section of happily married, divorced, divorced and remarried and single women currently in long-term relationships.

I found that divorced women certainly have a lot of wisdom in assessing the reasons for their failed relationships. All were determined to not fall into the same traps in their current relationships and were making every effort to approach them differently. I found it most interesting that out of all the differences in opinions, the two things that all the women agreed on was the absolute need for TRUST and RESPECT in their relationships. They all felt without these two vital ingredients that passion, good sex and successful communication will never happen in a relationship.

TRUST BUSTERS

I asked the women to define *trust* for me and tell me the reasons why they felt it was essential to a relationship. One woman said, "I trust my husband implicitly because I always know he wouldn't hurt me for the world." She went on to explain that when you have this kind of trust going for you in a relationship, it makes you feel positive about everything else your spouse does. "You don't have to be *suspicious* of him and constantly question his motives," she said. "You know that he is always doing things with your ultimate happiness in mind and that's very powerful in maintaining love."

All the women wanted to feel assured that their spouses would put their interests above all else and support them through the stressful times like illness and family problems as well as the good times. They felt that this had to be accomplished through complete honesty and a willingness for a couple to share their innermost feelings. And only after they felt the security of being able to totally trust their mate, would intimacy and passion be able to grow and flourish between them.

I asked them if this worked both ways and they all said "of course." However, a lot of these women and others I have interviewed felt that women were a lot more honest, open, and trustworthy in general, than men were in relationships. They felt it was not easy to find a man who fulfilled these basic expectations and it was the reason many of them got divorced and had not remarried. Probing further, I asked them to describe some of the things they felt contributed to the lack of trust in the other person. This is a summary of the issues we discussed which they felt had a direct bearing on trust in a relationship:

1. **If A Partner Lies To You** – In the normal course of human interaction, all of us are guilty of telling some "white" lies and even an occasional *whopper*. Many times we lie to avoid hurting the other person's feelings, or to spare them in some way from another's hurts. But it's the intentional lies about important issues between the couples, or when one partner becomes aware that the other frequently lies in his interactions with them as well as other people, that can build up some serious relationship blocks. We enter the marriage wholeheartedly believing that the one thing we should be able to count on is our spouse's total honesty with us. And if we begin to realize that he's frequently lying about things to us, every other part of the relationship begins to suffer. Doubt is a horrible feeling because it breaks down trust. We feel that if he lied to us about where he was on a particular evening, then how can we believe him when he says he loves us? And when he's making love to us, we can't help but hold back out of resentment for his dishonesty. Lies have an inherently mushrooming effect. And it's essential that we make the other person aware of how destructive they are in the big picture.

So it is very, very important to try and establish total honesty between you and your spouse/partner. Both parties must sit down and explore the ramifications of what price the lies will cost the relationship. *Women have to strongly tell men that if they can't trust their word, they are going to lose respect for them and at some point it's going to be irreparable.* Truth has got to be a #1 priority in your relationship. And it can't be emphasized enough because the whole basis of a successful relationship is ultimately based on trust. Without it, growth and love will become impossible.

2. **Baggage** – Baggage represents emotional residue from past problems that we bring into the relationship. And it often has a negative connotation.

LADIES, START YOUR ENGINES!!

Ex-wives, kids, ex-lovers and stressful family relationships are, to name just a few, pieces of baggage we carry with us. And if the couples are being overwhelmed with too many of these at once, it makes concentration on their present relationship difficult because they are expending all their energies cleaning up the baggage from the past. It also goes hand and hand with trust. When women begin to assign blame to their spouses for failures in their previous marriages, they begin to lose trust in them, fearing that the past will repeat itself. This is why *it is vital that the couples work through the past baggage BEFORE committing to their own permanent relationship.* Women have got to examine that past baggage and come to a realization that no matter what the prior circumstances were, they can trust their husbands in their own interactions. The kind of suspicious thinking that often occurs in marriages with baggage is as follows: "If he cheated on his ex-wife, then he's capable of cheating on me." And once this kind of mistrust has been firmly established in one partner's mind, it's going to become very difficult to build any meaningful foundation in the relationship in any other area.

These issues of trust are the ones that must be thoroughly examined and resolved early on in the relationship or else that nagging lack of trust will eventually become a self-fulfilling prophecy. He may adopt the defensive attitude that "I might as well go out and cheat if I'm going to be accused of it anyway." And so the cycle of mistrust prevents any possibility of successful bonding in the future.

3. **Manipulation** – This is a negative behavior which is utilized by both men and women to get what they want in terms of desired behavior from the other. We resort to it, because in our minds it is easier than having to argue, nag or yell to get what we want. We feel that we aren't being so blatant when we manipulate. In fact, there are those who feel it is a clever way to attain their goals. The fallacy is that it under-estimates the intelligence of the other person. Manipulation is usually very transparent and arouses the partner's anger for under-estimating him. Another danger in this kind of behavior is that it utilizes lying and deceit and therefore can lead to the same damage in our relationships as we feel an outright confrontation would. Here is an example of manipulation:

A husband tells his wife that he is going out on Wednesday night to play poker with his buddies. She doesn't want him to go because she doesn't like his friends and would rather have him home with her. So instead of communicating honestly with him and risking a blow up over the situation, she finds it easier to resort to manipulation. On Wednesday night she becomes "ill" with a headache, stomach ache or menstrual problems. He isn't happy about it but feels that he must stay home with her or he'll look like a complete louse. However, he suspects that she is playing a game with him but doesn't want to risk looking like he doesn't care. So he stays home but he is resentful and sulky. Not only this, but her little charade has undermined his trust in her.

So who won here? Nobody. She may have WON THE BATTLE but she LOST THE WAR. Her actions put a wedge of distrust between them and were self-defeating. With manipulation, everyone is the loser. Instead, she should have aired her real feelings without placing guilt or blame on him. They needed to discuss the problem utilizing all the positive techniques in communication we have talked about in previous chapters. They could have easily reached a compromise or a resolution. What they got instead was an unsatisfying evening and an erosion of trust. Manipulation also makes the partner feel that his power has been taken away and this causes further resentment. Employing deceit of any kind to gain a temporary victory will only end in a stunning defeat for the relationship.

4. **Infidelity** – CHEATING ON A SPOUSE IS THE ULTIMATE BETRAYAL. There isn't anything worse a spouse could do to not only ruin the present trust, but erase hope of ever regaining it in the future. Most marriages do not survive infidelity. However, those that do require an enormous amount of work toward repair and unconditional forgiveness. It also adds the very difficult burden on the betrayer of convincing his spouse that he can be trusted again. I think that in reality, this is nearly impossible. Because no matter how clean his record is from then on, his wife is always wondering "will he do it again?" I am not saying that it is always impossible, but I feel that the quality of the relationship will probably never be what it was before that act of betrayal took place.

However, there are couples whose marriages have successfully survived an infidelity. But in nearly every case, the couples have sought counseling to help them put the pieces of their lives back together. The depths of anguish and despair which result from an act of infidelity will take many months or even years to overcome. Re-establishing trust will be a very large task and require commitment, patience and the ongoing guidance of a competent marriage counselor. And most of all, the couple must determine that there is enough love left between them to really want their marriage to continue.

5. **Not Trusting In Each Other's Judgement** – Throughout a marriage, situations will constantly arise where you or your spouse will have to make decisions based on your judgements. This is where respect and trust become one and the same. We must trust each other's judgements and

respect them. We may not always agree on the same course of action, but showing respect for the other's judgement is important to maintain self-esteem in both parties. We have to trust that no matter what, our partner has our best interests at heart. To invalidate that is like saying the other person acts only out of self-interest. And this can be very hurtful and damaging to our relationships. If we don't trust in each other's judgements, we are saying that we don't respect how they think. And there's no faster way to damage another person's self–esteem than by continually giving off that message.

None of us consciously enters into a long-term relationship with a person we don't trust. But sometimes, as the relationship goes on, we may begin to feel less and less trust in the other person. If this is the case, then you'll need to do some serious thinking as to why this is happening. The causes have to be identified and remedial work must begin, because it's a very destructive position to be operating from. Why have you lost trust in him? Is he lying, cheating or doing things that are directly hurting you? No matter how unpleasant these issues may be to deal with, *the WORST thing to do is go into denial and let his behavior continue unquestioned.* When something as important as trust seems to be slipping away, it's a good idea to go for counseling to get things back on track. Loss of trust will CRIPPLE a marriage. And unlike an engagement or unmarried relationship where you can walk away, it's a lot tougher to do in a marriage. So there has to be some immediate attention and work applied to solve the problem and help rebuild that trust. The women in our discussion groups all agreed with me that the best way to resolve the problem when there is an erosion of trust in a relationship is to:

A. IDENTIFY THE SPECIFIC INSTANCES WHERE TRUST WAS SLIPPING AWAY IN YOUR RELATIONSHIP.

B. ASCERTAIN WHO IS CAUSING THE PROBLEM OR IF IT'S SOMETHING YOU'RE BOTH DOING.

C. EACH PARTNER SHOULD WRITE DOWN, IN DETAIL, WHAT THE PROBLEMS ARE AND HOW YOU FEEL THEY ARE AFFECTING YOUR RELATIONSHIP.

D. GET TOGETHER AND DISCUSS YOUR FINDINGS, CITING EXAMPLES OF HOW THE LACK OF TRUST IS GOING BEYOND A SINGLE ISSUE AND CARRYING OVER INTO OTHER AREAS OF YOUR RELATIONSHIP.

E. WORK ON THE ISSUES WHICH ARE WITHIN YOUR CAPABILITIES OF FINDING COMPROMISES FOR OR RESOLVING.

F. COME TO A MUTUAL DECISION TO GO FOR COUNSELING FOR THE ISSUES YOU VEHEMENTLY DISAGREE ON AND ARE BEYOND THE SCOPE OF YOUR ATTEMPTS AT RESOLUTION.

THE RELATED ISSUE OF RESPECT

The group of women defined respect this way:

Respect is in the mind and in the heart.

Respect is always non-judgment and a shared philosophical way of living.

Without respect, love can never take place between two people.

So what does this actually translate into in terms of everyday living? Well, first of all, when you respect someone you VALUE them as a person and therefore you also value their NEEDS. Respect is also when you truly admire a person for their qualities of honesty, fairness, ability to love and be loved and their other strengths. Women respect the strength men show in their protectiveness and caring for them and their families. Our Mothers taught us as children that if a man respects his mother he will also do the same for his wife. We teach our children how to respect us and others. We place great value on it in all cultures because we inherently realize how important respect is in forming successful relationships. When we respect someone it's easy to trust them with our love and our feelings.

The following is a list formulated by the women in our discussion group about the kinds of trust we form in relationships:

1. Respect For A Person's Accomplishments – Many women are initially attracted to a man because he is powerful and accomplished in his job. We are attracted to power and often the wealth that accompanies a successful man. However, there are women who fall in love with rich and powerful men because of what they REPRESENT. However, it does not necessarily mean that that's who they ARE. And if that person should lose his power or money, the relationship will suffer because her respect was for THOSE THINGS and not the man, himself.

So it is highly important for women to make an honest distinction between the two to avoid problems later on. A woman who falls in love with a poor man can usually adjust quite well if he gains wealth and power later on, but the reverse situation is often devastating to the relationship. We must first have respect for the man's values, kindness, strength or whatever his inherent qualities are–rich or poor. We must learn that the respect for power and the respect for the man as a person lie in two different arenas. Naturally, it is possible to have both. *But it's important to remem-*

ber that a man ISN'T his job. He must be loved and respected for who he is as a person and not confused with what he represents.

2. Respect and Passion – The two go hand in hand. You can't experience passion for anyone you don't respect. If you don't respect who they are, you'll never be able to work up any passion for them or be inspired by them. Women who lose respect for their husbands ultimately lose their ability to have any kind of passionate or fulfilling sex with them. In fact, many of these relationships become sexless when all respect is gone. Men may operate on a slightly different level. They can sleep with a bunch of women they don't respect, however, they very seldom end up married to one. So on some level, the sexes do come to an agreement on this issue. All of the women in our group who were divorced felt that the gradual loss of respect for their partners over time directly contributed to their loss of sexual feelings for them.

What male behaviors make a woman lose respect for her man? His lack of honesty, his lack of loyalty, his inability to communicate and his demonstrable lack of respect in his treatment of her are to name just a few. But one thing is for sure. When it happens, the first area of dysfunction will show up in their sexual interaction. So couples need to work on and be diligent about keeping their respect level for one another growing.

3. Respect and Communication – When one partner loses respect for the other, he also loses the desire to have good communication with him. This is because a lack of respect breeds apathy for the partner. If she doesn't respect him, then she won't respect his opinions or views about anything else either. She will turn her attention to her kids, parents, friends or fixate on some idol like a movie or sports superstar, or a public figure in the community as the recipient of her respect. This lessens his self-esteem and breeds counter-resentment in him. And the less they communicate out of the bedroom will mean that there's no meaningful communication happening between them in the bedroom. In sex especially, women still want a man they can *look up* to. Even though women have made great strides in their own individual liberties over the past hundred years, most still like being the *weaker sex* and dominated in the bedroom. And trying to make love to a man you don't respect doesn't work for a woman. It goes against all her inherent instincts.

4. Respect Not Fear – In previous generations, a woman's respect for a man often contained the element of fear. *A woman was to know her place in the relationship* and marriages contained strict guidelines as to the appropriate behaviors of men and women. Naturally, the men had a much better deal. They enjoyed more freedoms and were allowed a wide berth in their behavior. Thank goodness we women have become much more equal in our relationships nowadays and are constantly making strides for total equality. But I feel that, especially in this generation, there's still a lot of crossing over and confusion in the roles of spouses.

I think that many women still have an element of fear in certain aspects of their marriages which they mistakenly confuse with respect. For example, we often had the most respect for teachers we feared a little. We were careful not to cross the line in certain behaviors. This applies to some relationships. It is still surprising to me when some women say that *their husbands will not allow them to go out at night with girlfriends or won't allow them to go to work.* When asked why they accept these kinds of restrictions, they say they "respect" his wishes in certain areas. But their acceptance is not based on respect for him, it's actually based on FEAR OF HIM. The price of fighting for their rights must be too great to pay, so they present it as a positive instead of a negative. Now this might have worked 30 years ago when male-female roles were rigidly defined, but not today.

This form of "respect" eats away at the very foundations of a marriage. When these women open their eyes and see what kind of lives other women are living, they have got to feel resentment for their spouse. And with that resentment goes all the other marriage–busting baggage that we've discussed before. This kind of domination will eat away a woman's self-esteem and keep her in a submissive position throughout the marriage. And it only gets worse. The bottom line is that women have got to examine their relationships carefully and assess them truthfully. Maybe they marry men they fear because their mothers did. We learn from the examples our parents set. But, whatever the reasons, *love and passion CANNOT grow in an atmosphere of fear.* Respect has it's roots in honesty, integrity and sound values. Fear can never evoke any of these things. It's important to know and recognize the difference.

FORGIVENESS

We have just covered a great deal of ground in describing the kinds of behaviors which erode relationships and lead to a loss of passion and love. We have talked about lying, manipulation, negative arguing and much more. And the fact is that, in all relationships, one or more of these negative interactions are bound to occur with some frequency. The intent of this book is to teach you how to work at preventing future occurrences. However, the reality is that we can never completely prevent or eradicate every one of these problems in our relationships. So, what do we do about the wrongs and hurts that have taken place or will take place in the future?

Cutting through it all, *the one thing that is absolutely essential in keeping love and nurturing alive throughout our lifetimes is the ability to FORGIVE.* Without forgiveness we cannot move on and heal our relationships. However, total forgiveness is not always an easy thing to accomplish. The following are brief explanations about the essence of forgiveness, starting with the more negative aspects of attempting to forgive and progressing to the most positive:

1. Getting Even Instead Of Forgiving – One way many of us deal with the pain and anger inflicted by a wrongful act against us is to set out on a course of getting even. We do this for two reasons:

a. We feel it will lessen the pain and hurt we are experiencing by giving the wrong-doer a "dose of his own medicine."

b. We are unwilling or don't know how to forgive–so we choose a path of revenge, somehow believing it will "set things right" again.

People who use revenge as a method of alleviating their hurt and anger cannot foresee that these acts will eventually backfire and bring about more pain and anguish for themselves. Our pride gets in the way and we choose to punish and withdraw from the other person thinking we will heal ourselves by this method. But how mistaken we are. When we avoid dealing with the initial problem and don't resolve it by ultimately forgiving that person, true healing can never take place. Also by bearing a grudge or seeking revenge, we are utilizing our energies for negative results. These behaviors will exhaust and strip us of our positive powers that can be used to heal.

Revenge and hate keep us suspicious and ultimately destroy all trust in the relationship. We will lose the war in exchange for attaining a hollow victory by hurting the wrong-doer. It can't be emphasized enough how destructive this is in terms of the long-term relationship. We need to abandon this kind of thinking and realize how childish and self-defeating it is. It is never healthy to live in an atmosphere of hate and vengeance. It will kill any remaining love and trust we have left in us.

2. Conditional Forgiveness Is Not TRUE Forgiveness – When we assume a role of superiority and try to strike a bargain in exchange for our forgiveness, this is not really forgiveness at all. The attitude of "I'll forgive you IF and WHEN" will make the wrong-doer suffer loss of dignity, humiliate him and perpetuate his guilt. This is what we often refer to as "emotional blackmail." Forgiveness should never be offered on these grounds. Forgiveness has to be unconditional. When we forgive, we offer empathy and make allowances for the hurt that was incurred. We admit that we are human too, and we are certainly capable of the same thing. Then we can make a fresh start, moving on with compassion and without the need for revenge. Our love will also become renewed. And with it, the revelation that the unresolved hate and anger is not only killing our relationship, but is killing US personally.

3. Forgiveness Means Breaking Down Old Walls – When a person is hurt deeply, it's a natural reaction to pull back emotionally and avoid the possibility of further hurt. Unfortunately, by reacting this way it will also stifle all your positive emotions. And what happens is that you become so anesthetized to all feelings that you couldn't possibly forgive anybody in that state. In order to avoid this, it takes the courage to do the opposite. You have to open yourself up emotionally and accept the feeling of discomfort by processing your own anger and fear. And when you become a *feeling* person again, you'll have the ability to empathize with the transgressor and begin the process of forgiveness. But you'll need to forgive yourself first. Forgive and feel. This is what you must do for yourself before you'll be able to do it for another.

4. Forgiving and Forgetting – You often hear people say "I can forgive, but I will never forget what was done to me." They think, that by constantly recalling the past transgression, it will somehow shield them from it happening again. This is also not a case of truly forgiving. As long as a person keeps the memory of that hurt alive in himself, true forgiveness has not occurred. Forgetting a transgression does not mean that we have accepted the responsibility for the wrong doing or condoned it. Often we believe that the wrong-doer should suffer some long-term punishment or offer some repentance for his act. But this is getting back into the same old pattern of revenge. By not allowing the past to remain in the past, we simply reinforce our own discomfort and resentment and keep our suspicions fulminating.

5. Forgiveness Requires Love – Attaining a state of unconditional forgiveness requires love. When we love, we can look upon the wrong-doer as worthy and separate his action from who he is as a person. We may never fully understand why he did what he did. But it has to be set aside. With the strength of our love and the realization that a loving relationship requires trust and respect to survive, we will need to forgive without any conditions attached. We will understand through love the importance of being able to trust again. We need to let go of the illusions that people must be perfect and accept their imperfections and vulnerabilities just as we do their strengths. Letting go of the pain will free us to move ahead and enjoy our lives in countless creative ways. We will be able to channel our negative energies into positive energy that creates hope and love in our lives.

6. Learning How To Forgive – Once we truly internalize WHY it is so important to forgive, we need to learn HOW to forgive. Sometimes it is fairly easy to forgive a minor transgression and get on with our lives. Other times, it is the hardest thing in the world to do. But we MUST forgive, if we truly want our relationship to grow with love.

The first step in forgiving is to put the problem into perspective and separate it from the perpetrator. We have to remember that we are all human and we are entirely capable of doing wrong against another as someone does to us. We need to view the wrong-doer as no better or worse than ourselves. There needs to be a suspension of judgement and adjustment of our attitudes so that we do not see ourselves as the "good" and the wrong-doer as the "bad" person. We need to separate his ACTIONS from who HE IS. He may have done something unfair and hurtful, but that is no reason to judge him in totality as being a bad or evil person. If we don't do this, then we will always attach suspicion and distrust to that person in all future dealings. It will prevent healing and future growth for both parties in the relationship. We need to apply our open and honest communication in dealing with the act and come to a resolution between the parties as unjudgmentally as possible. And when we do, it must be UNCONDITIONAL. The act must be put behind us because true forgiveness has taken place.

CONTROL

Our discussion group felt that the issue of control played a large part in the topics we are talking about in this chapter. It's a type of behavior which stems from a person's own insecurities or it can be a direct effect of their jealousy, lack of respect or lack of trust in another person. But no matter what causes it, control is an attempt of one person to make the other behave in certain ways which allow the controller to feel secure or superior. But, as with any negative behavior, control will ultimately lead to an unbalancing of the relationship, eroding healthy communication and stunting its growth. It usurps the positive passion which should be used to strengthen our love and twists it into a *passion for control*.

Controlling A Partner's Interactions With Others – If a man is basically insecure about his wife's love for him (with or without just cause), he may attempt to control who she sees, where she goes and what she does. He attempts to LIMIT her scope of interactions because he thinks:

a. she might meet another man she finds more attractive than him

b. she could hear other's opinions about him which he perceives as pos-

110

sibly threatening to their relationship.

Since a woman's role, traditionally, is often more passive in relationships, she may try to counter-control through more manipulative means, knowing that any outright power play will be met by his overwhelming objection. For example, she may tell him that she is going to a cooking class with a few girlfriends, when she is actually going out to dinner with them.

Many women also see themselves as having very little power because they are dependent on a man's income. When a woman isn't earning her own income, it automatically puts the man in a position of power and control. Women placed in this position of dependency also attempt to control through some of these more *subtle* means:

Control By Having Children – Many insecure women try to establish an *escape proof* environment for their husbands by consciously or unconsciously locking him into a family complete with kids, a house, a mortgage and activities that revolve solely around the family. They attempt manipulation through their kids. The husband is told that he can't go golfing, for example, because she needs help with the baby, or the kids need him at their activities–or any number of excuses to keep him home and *accounted for.*

Often in re-marriages, where the husband or wife has kids by a former spouse, the present wife will insist on having their own baby right away in an attempt to *compete* with the time he spends with his own kids. It's also a way of adjusting her own *comfort level* by reducing the threat she feels from the bond he maintains with his ex-wife because of their kids. By providing a *new family* of their own with all it's inherent responsibilities, she is taking his time and energies away from the old ones. She feels it adds more *permanence* and *security* to their marriage. She figures that the last thing he wants is to have another divorce and be responsible for added alimony and child support payments. So by having children of their own, it gives her the leverage she needs to keep him permanently at her side.

Control By Guilt – Insecure women often use their feminine wiles and play the role of the "weak woman" to control their husbands. We all know women who are continually "ill" with a host of vague physical and emotional problems which keeps their husbands glued to their side. Instead of standing up for what they want in terms of time and expectations, they find it easier to get what they want by using *passive-aggressive* tactics. If he calls and tells her he has to work late, arousing her suspicions, she will manipulate him into coming home with her tears and pleas. She might say that she can't possibly handle the kids alone, or tell him she had planned a "special" dinner. She'll use whatever it takes to put him on the defensive and feel guilty about his absence. How many times have we heard or used these phrases: "The kids need you more than your boss does," or "I really need you home with me because I'm having a rough day," or any other number of guilt-inducing and loyalty-testing tactics.

Control By Withholding Sex – A female friend once said to me, "When you think about it, what REAL power do we have over our husbands? If they decide to withhold money, tear up our credit cards or go to a bar after work– what recourse do we have? Leave home with no money or throw tantrums every day–or what? The truth is that we have very little in the way of options. So what most of us do is close our legs until he relents."

And what do I think about what she said? I think that this is the #1 most common way women use to exert control over men. This is one of the most effective ways of showing our disapproval and "hitting him where it hurts." Sooner or later, he's going to give in on his position, because this is the one thing he wants that he can't force you to do. However, even though it can be a mighty effective tactic, it's something that, if continually used, will "lose the war" for you in the long run. It's going to make him extremely resentful and force him to build emotional walls around himself to handle his feelings of rejection. And this can easily lead to a situation where his passion for you diminishes to the point where your *withholding tactic* is met by his total indifference.

OPERATING FROM A POSITION OF WEAKNESS

The most obvious problem with control is that even if it accomplishes your immediate goals, in the long run it's going to build a wall of resentment between spouses which will become impenetrable. In attempting to *put the squeeze on him* through whatever means, it will ultimately *squeeze* the love and passion out of your relationship. *Either sex KNOWS when they are being manipulated.* They may succumb to it but consider it *dirty fighting.* They will not only hate what you're DOING but eventually hate YOU for doing it.

The alternative to utilizing some or all of the control tactics listed above is to switch from a position of weakness to a position of strength. And to accomplish this, *we MUST BEGIN working to change our insecurities.* We must recognize that our perceived need for using this type of behavior is being generated from the insecurity within ourselves as well as within our relationship. Begin by identifying those factors which are making you uneasy about your relationship. Ask yourselves the following questions:

1. Do you feel that unless you control your husband's activities, he'll be more likely to leave the relationship?

2. Do you think that no matter what your problems are, your husband would never leave you because of the children?

3. Do you feel like you're really not meeting his emotional needs?

4. Do you frequently act unresponsively during sex?

5. Do you feel that most women out there are more attractive and sexy than you? More educated? More fun?

6. Do you feel like you are intellectually inferior to him?

Be very very honest with yourself and take responsibility for the areas in which your insecurities are putting a strain on your relationship. And instead of sitting there and stewing about the problems, DO some remedial work on the things that are making you insecure and unhappy. For example:

1. If you feel a better education would improve your self–esteem, research the college "extension" courses (for adults) offered at a nearby college or university.

- Make a habit of reading the newspaper or magazines like "Time" which give a summarized overview of what's going on in the world.
- Make a point of visiting your library once or twice a week to read up on topics of interest to you.
- Watch educational programs on TV instead of soap operas. The Discovery Channel offers a variety of fascinating topics.
- Join a book review club to stimulate your reading where you can participate in discussions which sharpen your intellect.
- Instead of listening to rock music when driving someplace, play motivational tapes or tapes of current books on audio.
- Read and learn about a subject your husband or lover is interested in that you know very little about.

2. If you are unhappy with your body and sexual image, get yourself on a regular program of diet and exercise.

- Ask a friend or your husband to be your exercise "buddy" and go work out together and constantly encourage each other.

- And when you lose the first 10 pounds, reward yourself with a new dress or some sexy underwear.

3. If you feel that you aren't included in enough of your husband's activities, learn to do some of the things he likes so you'll be able to join him.

- If golf is one of his passions, take some lessons for yourself. And when you have acquired the basic skills of the game, ask him to take you out on the course to play a few rounds.
- If he's a computer nut, take a few courses so you will be able to understand the basics. Get on the Internet together or challenge him to some computer games.
- If he's into running, train by yourself until you're able to keep up with him for a mile or even half a mile.

Keep in mind that nobody wants to be around another person who is constantly defensive due to their insecurities. This is how you lose a man. And tying him up with a bunch of kids or a big home or manipulating his time won't keep him in the marriage, if he is basically miserable. The marriage is about THE TWO OF YOU–your love, your passion, your sexual intimacy and your sharing of yourselves. These are things generated from within–not things you can harness.

THE NEED FOR SPACE

We have talked in-depth about the need for communication, nurturing and closeness to intensify passion and romance. But the need for space is equally as important. We are all human beings who have an inherent need for *alone time*. We all need our share of friends and interests outside of our relationship. It is normal and healthy. We use our friends as support and our interests to keep us growing intellectually and emotionally as human beings. And although our relationship is our priority in life, it does not mean that it should exclude everything else. This is unhealthy. It is smothering behavior that will snuff the passion out of our relationships. Passion is fueled by external, as well as internal, factors. Marriage should never put an end to our personal growth. And to keep growing, we all need our personal space and time.

If he chooses to play poker one night, accept the fact that it is healthy and normal for him to want to relax with his buddies. Don't take it as a situation where he has made a *choice* of his friends over you. Use your *free night* as an opportunity to read, do your nails, take a luxurious bubble bath, study or rent one of those *female* type movies like *Beaches*, which he didn't want to see. This is how a confident and empowered woman acts. She also knows that when her husband gets home and is greeted by a loving, cheerful woman instead of a whiny and resentful one, he'll be delighted to see you. He might even find that he actually prefers skipping one of those poker games to spend the evening with you. This is real empowerment.

However, *space* should not be used as a means of avoidance. This is something totally different. The whole point of having *individual space* in a relationship is to ADD to the relationship NOT TO AVOID it. This is an important distinction which needs to be weighed when evaluating both of your motives. And if couples get to the point in their relationship where they are truly avoiding each other, it indicates the need for immediate counseling. As with anything else in your relationship, there has to be a healthy balance operating between you.

Here are some examples of using space as an excuse to avoid the other partner.

1. A partner says he needs to go on a vacation alone because he is feeling "trapped."

2. Either partner insists on going out to bars or clubs several nights a week with the *boys* or the *girls*.

3. A partner is in the habit of getting up from the dinner table night after night and going straight to the TV set or computer where he spends the entire evening without making any further effort to communicate with the other.

4. A spouse continually avoids involving himself in any facet of his children's' lives or activities because he needs to *do his own thing*.

5. A partner suddenly develops the habit of going out for several evenings each week and gives no explanation other than he *"needs his space."*

While listening to a radio talk show, a woman complained that her husband was demanding that he didn't have to be accountable for time he spent away from the family because he needed his *space*. To which the radio psychologist responded—"What's her name?" Her remark cut right to the heart of the matter. There is a big difference between *healthy space* in relationships and *avoidance space* because the relationship is not working. The concept of establishing "personal space" must be a negotiable thing. No partner has the right to ever threaten to leave the relationship unless he is given his "space." And if you are in a situation where this happens, you really only have two options:

1. Let him walk – never allow yourself to be held hostage by this unreasonable ultimatum.

2. If you aren't ready to call it quits, then you must insist on counseling to see if your relationship is capable of being repaired. If he refuses, then unfortunately his actions tell you that he has no interest in continuing the relationship anyway.

CHAPTER 8

JEALOUSY

JEALOUSY AND PASSION

Many people think of jealousy and passion as going together. Jealousy is a "fiery" feeling that usually stems from great passion for someone. It is a normal feeling which we all have experienced to some degree during our lives. The thing that is NOT normal is when we act on our jealousy in extreme or irrational ways. When this happens, our behavior becomes destructive and self–defeating. We are going to discuss ways of making sure jealousy doesn't consume us and ruin our relationships.

REASONS FOR JEALOUSY

1. INSECURITY – When we love someone deeply, we tend to become possessive. We become afraid that the other friendships or kinds of relationships our loved one shares with anyone other than ourselves might take him away. We become frightened at the possibility of losing the love we have created. Often we internalize the feeling, thinking that no one else could understand or help us in our struggle. But what's really behind these feelings is our insecurity about the relationship. And this is what becomes expressed as jealousy.

An insecure person might continually be thinking, "I don't like him spending so much time with his friends. He has more fun with them than with me. How am I going to compete?" Or "I can't stand the way he's always doting over his mother. He talks to her more than he does with me. Why can't he just be happy with my love and attention?" Insecure people are at war with themselves. And their problems begin to mushroom when the jealous person begins expressing their jealousy in different forms of anger towards the objects of their jealousy. This situation will eventually wear down the positives in the relationship and kill the passion in it. To change this kind of destructive behavior, the jealous person must channel his positive energies back into the relationship.

The best way to deal with insecurity is to make an honest assessment of the problem. Is there a valid reason for your jealousy–like if he's actually flirting or cheating? Is he abandoning you for others? If not, where is your insecurity coming from? Why do you feel that your relationship might fall apart so easily? Start communicating with your partner to get at the root of the problem. Turn those energies into building passion and closeness between you, not eroding it. It will take a lot of introspection and self-discipline, but, once you begin identifying the nature of your insecurities, you can begin to strengthen the weak areas in your relationship.

As you become more secure in the relationship, you will find that the jealousy lessens to a great extent. You can also become a lot more detached in being able to analyze where the feelings are originating from. ALWAYS KEEP IN MIND THAT JEALOUSY IS A USELESS AND DESTRUCTIVE EMOTION. It will keep you from working on the real issues which need improvement. Jealousy paralyzes you, preventing positive action which could help create solutions for you. Recognize that clinging to your jealousy will only destroy yourself. Jealousy will take a big effort to conquer, but it's not impossible.

2. LOW SELF-ESTEEM – When a person thinks so little of himself that he spends all his energy comparing himself unfavorably with others, he is bound to become a very jealous individual. He may internalize his feelings and suffer daily in silence because he feels helpless about ever being able to compete. It becomes very apparent that this is a problem caused and carried on solely within the person. It is an internal problem whose roots lie in the lack of self-esteem. These people are continually measuring themselves against others with thoughts like, "Oh, she's so pretty. I know he wishes I had a face and figure like hers. He's probably secretly in love with her." Or, "I know I could never be as smart or as charming as she. I hate it when she's around, because I know my husband is always comparing me with her."

In most cases, probably 99% of these thoughts have no real basis in fact. They are imagined by the person with low self-esteem and serve no constructive purpose. Instead, they keep her down, insecure and withdrawn. This is going to have a huge impact on her relationship with her husband and those around her. I can't think of a more tormented way of going through life than to be jealous of everybody you come into contact with. To view everyone as a potential threat to your relationship will paralyze you into withdrawal and depression.

So how does one go about correcting the enormous problem of low self-esteem? Surely the first place to start is by admitting you have an all encompassing problem with the way you see yourself. The next is to fully realize how destructive it is to you and your partner and all your interactions. And once you recognize it as YOUR problem, you can take some pos-

118

itive measures to help improve your self-image. Sit down and give some serious thought about the areas you feel deficient in and how they are impacting your relationship in a negative way. The seriousness of these problems and how they are affecting your happiness and that of your spouse will serve as your motivation to make positive changes. The physical problems like *being overweight or feeling unattractive CAN BE CORRECTED.*

We talked about specific steps you can take to build up your self-esteem in a previous chapter. Getting yourself on a program of regular exercise and a healthier diet can be a very enjoyable venture. Joining a health club is something you can do for yourself that will make you look and feel better. You will probably meet some new female friends there and form some exercise buddy support systems as an added benefit. Treat yourself to a makeover at a department store or get your hair re-styled at a beauty parlor. And as you begin to look and feel better, reward yourself with some new clothes or cosmetics to keep you motivated. These are all measures that are not that difficult to accomplish and produce results in a relatively short time.

However, a more serious lack of self-esteem is often rooted in childhood and you may come to the conclusion that you need counseling to overcome your negative self-image problems. If this is the case, then counseling is a wise investment toward your own well-being and future happiness, as well as for your relationship. Working through your problems and insecurities is not going to be a *piece of cake.* Uncovering and resolving deep-rooted hurts and childhood traumas is often a time-consuming and painful process. But you must remember that the end result will be worth every bit of your effort. Feeling well-adjusted, happy, and secure in your life is a goal that should supersede everything else. No person, man or woman, should go through their lives feeling constantly uncertain about themselves, or feeling depressed and hopeless. It is every person's inherent right to live their lives in happiness and with a sense of well-being.

3. JEALOUSY WITH GOOD REASON – If you are married or in a relationship with a man who is ostensibly a flirt or philanderer, then you have got to either get out of the relationship or start some serious dialogue with your partner to correct what's going on. Many women marry these type of men because of their own lack of self-esteem. They feel that the man has "done them a favor" by marrying them. Their thought processes follow this line: "He had many women in his life, but he chose me after all. I should feel lucky that he wanted me." Because of her insecurity, she never thought beyond this and realized that he did her no big favor. And now she's stuck

with a person who has a big character defect. He will, in all likelihood, make her life miserable.

There is a very important lesson to be learned here: If you don't love yourself, you will "settle" for anything that comes your way because deep down you don't feel worthy of true love. And if you don't change the way you think, you are going to experience utter despair every day of your life with the worthless man you settled for. A cheater has to be dealt with on uncompromising grounds. He must be told that you will never tolerate such behavior in your relationship and you must have the strength to mean what you say.

Couples who have experienced infidelity must get counseling to help repair the damages and help them to restore trust in their relationship, if they want to continue on together. Also, women with low self-images who settle for untrustworthy men, can also benefit from counseling to help them arrive at a place in their lives where they truly believe they are worthy of better than what they're getting. There are thousands of women out there who remain with spouses who beat them on a regular basis. And the reason they don't leave is because their self-esteem is so low that they believe that they are somehow *responsible for* or *deserve* the beatings. This is simply "unthinkable" to women who have a healthy sense of self-esteem, but sadly, it's a reality for those who don't. But it should serve as an important example of how serious the problem of low self-esteem can become and the depths of misery it can drag one's life down to. These are very complex and tough problems to overcome. *But no situation has to be considered as hopeless. With counseling and the love and support of friends and family, people can be healed by learning how to love themselves.*

PUTTING PERSPECTIVE ON OUR PROBLEMS

There are so many facets involved in keeping love and passion alive in our relationships that, at times, we may feel like we aren't capable of succeeding at all of them. However, keep in mind that all relationships will be negatively affected by the anger, frustration, jealousy and insecurities of the people in them from time to time. It is a part of life and can't be avoided altogether. We are not aiming for perfection in any of our human interactions. But, what we want to accomplish is gaining enough wisdom and insight to avoid the destructive, long-term negative interactions in our relationships. I hope that the issues and techniques we have discussed in this book will add enlightenment as to why these problems occur and teach you how to deal with them more effectively. We have heard testimony from women who are successfully making the love and passion in their relationships grow on a daily basis by utilizing the techniques in this book. And it is certainly within everyone's reach to achieve this goal.

It is vitally important that we learn to focus on the positives in our lives. One of the wisest pieces of advice ever to be handed down through the ages is "Count Your Blessings." When we are able to focus on the good in our lives and feel thankful for what we have achieved, it puts all the little problems and temporary setbacks in their true perspective.

For many years, I was actively involved in hospital volunteer work. It kept me in close contact with many hospitals in the different states in which I have lived. One day I happened to be doing some work in the children's' wing. As I walked down the hall, I peered into the various rooms. I saw brave little kids who were bald from chemotherapy still fighting valiantly to stay alive. I saw kids who were beaten and scarred from abuse. I saw children lying there unconscious with tubes in their noses. I saw children who had so many needles poked into them, their arms and legs looked like pin–cushions. To this day, the memory of their suffering brings tears to my eyes. And I thought on that day and have continued to think every day since then, "How fortunate I am to be a healthy and happy woman who is blessed with a wonderful family to love. So what if I have occasional problems? Compared to these kids and thousands like them all over the world, my life is a shining jewel. I ought to and will thank God for it everyday and do whatever I can to preserve it everyday of my life."

There is no better way to put your own problems into proper perspective than by becoming aware of the suffering of others. Just by walking down any street in a big city, you will see countless people who are sleeping under plastic bags to keep from freezing at night and scavenging food from garbage cans in alleyways. Think about the unfortunate people who are struck down by illness in the prime of their lives, or those who can't do something as simple as walking up a flight of steps. These are things we should all remember when battling the problems in our lives, large or small. It will help you to keep moving forward in love and gratitude. It will allow you to appreciate what you have been given and feel proud of the things you have worked hard for in your life. There is no greater means of uplifting yourself then when you "count your blessings."

CHAPTER 9

THE QUEST FOR PERFECTION

THE MYTH OF THE "PERFECT" MATE

I have talked with a lot of young men and women who have recently been in failed relationships. In trying to uncover some of the reasons why the parties drifted apart or just seemed to lose interest in each other, there is a disturbing undercurrent common to many of their stories. And that common thread is that people are judging their mates and the success of their relationships on false values. These values have more to do with what their mates look like and how sexy they perceive them to be, rather than on virtues such as loyalty, honesty, selflessness and the ability to love unconditionally.

One man said that his fiancee's "heavy thighs" turned him off to the point where he could no longer function sexually in the relationship. A young woman told me, that, although her boyfriend was "wonderful and fun to be with," he just wasn't "masculine enough" to keep her interested. Another man said that, even though the woman in his life was "wonderful, loving and giving," her small bust was such a problem for him that he found he was always looking elsewhere, wishing for a more voluptuous woman. And these statements weren't by any means isolated incidents. I hear the same kinds of complaints over and over again from people in their teens and on into their late forties. So, I have to ask myself this question: Is this the kind of criteria which people are basing their values for successful relationships on nowadays? Are we becoming so fixated on physical perfection that we are ignoring or not understanding the REAL qualities which it takes to make loving and long-term unions?

HOW THE MEDIA PROMOTES FALSE IDEALS

There has to be a reason why this trend of placing false values on people and relationships is occurring with greater frequency in our society. I feel that the culprits are the media and advertising. We are bombarded everyday by sensory stimuli which show people who have perfect bodies, perfectly white and even teeth, are super-macho or super-sexy and are capable of producing a mega-orgasm at any given second in their lives. It's really ludicrous isn't it? So why are we all BUYING INTO this picture of perfection? Men and women are NOT being represented REALISTICALLY by the media. We are being lied to and we are accepting it. The truth is, that every one of us is human and has flaws in certain areas. If we have a good heart, we still may have cellulite-ridden thighs. We all have our moments of cowardice. We all don't have an orgasm every time we make love. Many of us have crooked teeth or flabby bellies. But is that becoming the standard by which we choose or keep a mate in our relationships? The sad truth is that in many instances IT IS and the superficial values are increasingly becoming the standard by which younger and older people are basing their relationship choices.

So what does all this have to do with putting passion back into your relationship? Everything. As long as many of us continue to believe that only the "'beautiful" and "ideal" people are worthy of our love and commitment, we're going miss a lot of opportunities for finding potential mates with *real substance.* How many of us are going to pass on the man or woman who would have made our lives loving and complete, just because we judged her or him as not being "pretty enough" or "manly enough?" And there's also the very real danger of becoming disillusioned with the person you're married to because of all the so-called "beautiful people" out there you think you could have or deserve to have. This kind of thinking will breed discontent and promote fanciful thinking about how much happier you might be by dumping your "flawed mate" in exchange for a "perfect" one. And based on the high divorce rate in our society, it's obvious that many people aren't choosing partners with their hearts or keeping them for the same reason. These fleeting unions are happening because people are making bad choices based on bad values.

Why is it when *gorgeous couples* break up, everyone is so shocked? We hear comments like–"But they were so BEAUTIFUL together. They had it all–looks, money, a beautiful home, beautiful kids–what happened?" I'll tell you what happened. They had all the exterior trappings but lacked the compassion, true love, caring and commitment it takes to keep a relationship together. I am not saying that beautiful or rich people CAN't have lasting love or great relationships. Of course there are many people who have both. But when we are so focused on perfection that we don't even recognize the true qualities that we need to form a lasting relationship, we are never going to have it. And we must make the appropriate changes in our values and thinking to avoid becoming victims of this lie.

SEX, PASSION and THE MEDIA

The media–which includes TV, the movies and romance novels, to a lesser degree, are singlehandedly contributing to the most erroneous concepts of love and passion ever perpetrated on the public. What we see portrayed as sex and passion in the media are distorted caricatures of the same. In some films, we see two people who have perfect bodies coming together in a blur of candlelight and lace, sweating profusely and reaching the most intense of all simultaneous orgasms ever generated on the planet after just three minutes! Other films depict two degenerate and disgusting adults who hardly know each other, having sex with such physical intensity that it would rip the sex organs off of most normal people. In the most extreme cases, we see two people reach a violent climax, only to witness one of them savagely stabbing the other upon completion of the act. And today THIS is how we get our sexual images and reinforcement of sexual interaction as a steady diet.

Is it no wonder that it makes our young people either afraid of sexual commitment or so disillusioned by the real thing that their relationships fall apart? Is it surprising that men who learn about sex from the movies, suffer shattered egos when a woman fails to reach orgasm after two minutes of misguided and rough foreplay? Is it any wonder that women never learn to become orgasmic, because they can never respond the way their beautiful female idols in the movies do?

Movies and TV shows which portray casual or lurid sex are perpetrating a myth and offering up stereotyping at it's worst. This is NOT sex education. This is not how young people or adults should be learning their sexual values and techniques. And unfortunately, in today's' visually addicted society, this is probably the only place where most people are ever going to learn it from. And what about the worst of them all–the hard-core porn movies? Men are taught that the "harder they go at it, the more the woman will respond." They see women reaching orgasm merely at the sight of a ten inch penis. They see aggressive women delighting in depraved sex, group sex, sex with other women and violent sex. I find this very disturbing. And after men have spent years watching this misinformative garbage, what kind of chance do you think they have of learning what real sex is all about? How many failed relationships and years of anguish is it going to take to correct their thinking? Hopefully, with the love and understanding of a good partner, they will be able to separate the fantasy from the reality and get on the right track. But I think that these images stay with them for a life-time and subconsciously affect their sexual interactions.

Now, I am not advocating burning all of the steamy movies in America. I think that there are some which have their place in helping to stimulate people's sex lives. What I am saying, however, is that they are the wrong resources to LEARN about sex and how to PRACTICE it.

A BETTER PERSPECTIVE FOR SEXUAL BONDING

Part of the process of growing together sexually is by learning what your partner likes, how to stimulate them and how to share your love and passion to it's fullest. This takes time. It requires understanding, caring and love to make it happen. It takes the love and commitment of being able to work through those times when we can't achieve orgasm, or have lost some of our sex drive. The process of LOVING is ONGOING and involves many levels of communication. Many times it takes forgetting about the orgasm for a while and concentrating on the touching, caressing, and security that shared love brings. But it doesn't mean ditching the relationship when our false perceptions of what great sex should be aren't happening in our relationships. This is another misrepresentation in the movies where instant sex, instant orgasm, and instant passion just spontaneously HAPPENS for beautiful or sexy looking people. We see it, we buy into it, and we are CONSTANTLY DISAPPOINTED in ourselves and our partners when it doesn't happen for us too.

A BETTER WAY TO DEVELOP SOUND SEXUAL VALUES

How do we correct it? We go to the proper sources to learn about successful sex and passion. We should be in the bookstores or libraries reading up on the hundreds of knowledgeable books written by experts about how to make love, how to become sexually responsive and how to have lasting relationships. There are also many instructional videos which approach sexual education and sexual techniques on a wholesome level and present it with the respect it deserves. Fortunately, in today's society we have access to a lot of wisdom and great advice about how to educate ourselves sexually. And as we read about it, we should take the time to communicate what we've learned with our partners. Building our sexual and emotional communication with our partners requires time and continual dedication. And when we work towards building strong foundations, it will bring about a lifetime of successful sex and passion. Fabulous sex between partners is a result of good communication, letting go of anger, shared intimacy, respect, trust and committed love. This is where it's at!!

Of course we are all capable of having wild and orgasmic sex with another person. But does this assure us of a relationship that will be a happy one for the course of a lifetime? Is the great orgasm the measuring stick by which we judge the success of our relationships? No way. A continued successful sex-life and shared passion can only come from all the combined ingredients mentioned above. And if you don't believe it, you are going to spend a lifetime fraught with frustration and disappointment. My advice to people of all ages is to spend most of your time based in reality. Learn about building wonderful sex and passion with a real life person you're committed to. Start viewing movies and TV with a much more critical eye, based upon reality. Become accustomed to discerning fantasy from reality. You can look at perfection on the screen but if you spend all your time searching for it in real life, you're never going to find it. Unless you learn to accept your loved one with all his human flaws, you will experience disappointment after disappointment in quest of something which doesn't exist.

THE "HAVING IT ALL" SYNDROME

Another dangerous myth which is a product of modern day media is the depiction of the woman who "has it all." We are sold a bill of goods that it is entirely possible for women to be successful career people, great mothers, dutiful wives, trim, beautiful and fabulous sex partners. Oh really? So who's telling us this? Well to name a few, its the perfume companies, the movies, clothing manufacturers, cosmetic companies, cigarette companies and anyone else who is trying to sell you THEIR product with this myth. And what's happening? The women who believe it are ending up with anorexia, nervous breakdowns, loss of self-esteem, broken marriages and yuppie diseases like Epstein-Barr syndrome, because they have worn themselves out trying to achieve this lie. I don't know about you, but if I spent eight hours a day in a high-pressured job, came home and cared for my children and cleaned the house, I would NEVER have time for my husband much less be able to bolster the energy for great sex. An orgasm would probably kill me right there and then in my bed. It is ridiculous isn't it?

But the sad thing is that this "super-woman" myth is being taken seriously by too many women. In maximizing our expertise in one area like our careers, the other areas of child care, sex or whatever are going to suffer. Come on, ladies. You know they will. Nobody is a super-person. Most of us spend all of our time keeping our houses and kids well attended and have great difficulty finding an extra hour for our own needs. Yes, we can all use improvement in many areas. But think about how self-defeating it is to keep beating ourselves up because we can't fulfill this super-woman myth or EVEN a part of it. We need to learn to love ourselves and accept our own limitations as *normal* for us. Some women do combine career and marriage successfully. And if YOU CAN'T, so what? You should never strive to be a reflection of what somebody else says you ought to be. And this goes especially for some impersonal company that's only after your money anyway.

We need to learn to accept and cherish what we CAN do. And this means setting priorities for what's most important to us. If you are an excellent homemaker and mother, then give yourself the credit you deserve for your contributions in helping your family to function as a happy and secure unit. This is a major accomplishment all by itself. You should never feel diminished as a person because you have made your husband and your children your chosen *career*. There is a lot of wisdom in the statement that "success should never be measured in terms of money." Success should come from the inside—in terms of feeling a sense of accomplishment for a job well done. But it should never come at the expense of your personal health or happiness or that of your family.

CHAPTER 10

REAL LIFE LETTERS

REAL PEOPLE, REAL SUCCESSES

The following are letters which were sent to me from women of all ages and in all walks of life throughout the country. They serve to illustrate the issues which I have pointed out and were discussed in previous chapters and given practical advice which has been successful for them.

In the first few chapters, the problems of many women concerning a wide variety of issues were presented. However, I said that there was a small percentage of women who have found the secrets of how to keep the passion in their marriages alive. The letters below, printed in their entirety, demonstrate some fairly simple methods which have proven to be highly successful for the women who wrote them. These women are practicing in real life, the advice I have given in this book. You will see, first hand, how successfully they interact with their mates, and you'll learn how they have been able to keep reinventing the passion in their relationships. The letters are very encouraging because they show that it is possible to keep the fires of romance and passion alive in your relationship after many years.

MAKING SURE YOU HAVE "ADULT TIME"

The following letter is from Shelly, a happily married woman of 16 years who has four children all under the age of seven. What makes her so unique is that three of those children are triplets! Many of us have trouble finding alone time with our husbands with even two kids, so I felt this letter was a wonderful example of how it can be done against seemingly "impossible" odds.

Dear Jan,

When we first get a 'new toy' (applies to children and adults more loosely, as well) we play with it all the time, treasure it, and can't stand to be parted from it. Applying that same logic to new relationships...we just can't get enough of one another. Then life, jobs, kids and other relationships get in the way. The trick then becomes making that passion stay alive amongst all of life's divergences, because it's not new anymore. But I believe that if you really work at it-it will become even more exciting and much more intimate as time passes.

My husband and I have been married for 16 years now and I wouldn't trade him and our relationship for anything in this world. Secrets? No secrets. We work very hard at our marriage. We are best friends, partners and lovers. We still go out on "dates" together at least twice a month (not easy when you have small children)-no friends, no movies, just a place where we can talk without interruption. We celebrate every anniversary and renew our vows, light the candle that was on the altar, look at our wedding album- all that mushy, romantic stuff!!

We also make it a point to share the first ten minutes after he gets home from work with just each other. We sit and hold hands and talk with a timer on. Our kids know that this is "Mommy and Daddy's time" alone and they respect it. It helps them to see how much Mommy and Daddy love each other, and our relationship is important to us and to them. For those times when my husband is busy and preoccupied, I creep up on him with no clothes on and see how long it takes him to notice. And once he notices, he always manages to take a break!

Yours truly,

Shelly

PUTTING THESE PRINCIPLES INTO ACTION

This letter is not only touching, but it might inspire hope for many women who feel that children make it impossible to keep romance alive in their own marriages. It illustrates several crucial points that I have made in previous chapters.

1. The need for *alone time* with your spouse when you can nurture one another and really talk with one another.

2. Keeping each other and your relationship as the priority in your daily interactions.

3. You can be excellent parents but still have ground rules for the kids to follow that allow you and your husband to make time for one another. Her letter demonstrates how flexible the kids can be in this matter and how good it is for them to recognize parental time. Kids learn by example. And when they have been raised in an environment where the parents make time for their love and relationship, they will do the same thing when they get into their own relationships later in life. Nothing is "taken away" from the kids by what the parents are doing, rather a positive lesson is given back to them which enriches their lives as well.

4. The way this couple recalls their romantic and passionate times together is illustrated perfectly in the way they celebrate each anniversary. Looking at the wedding pictures, lighting the same candle–it's positively brilliant.

It's easy to see why this 16-year-old marriage is so successful, when you see how many things they do on a daily basis to keep it nurtured.

SEX AND BODY IMAGE

This letter is from Jeri, a divorced woman in her early fifties who had been married for over 20 years. She has some very insightful ideas as to why passion fades and sex gets put on the *back burner* from her experience during her own marriage. She segregates the topics and relates them with her own characteristic humor and insights:

Dear Jan,

If I have gained weight over the years or even sudden-ly-the urge to be butt naked in front of my husband (or lover if you're divorced) takes a lot of self-confidence. When you stop wearing nighties and avoid the bathroom mirror, which solution would you agree with?

a. exercise

b. eat sensibly

c. remove the mirrors

d. get past it-if he loves you only for your girlie body he's shallow.

e. accept it, but exercise and eat sensibly-and get a larger teddy, use candles, bubble baths and play Barry White music!!

Enjoying Vs. Pretending-If a woman only 'puts up' while she 'puts out' in the beginning of a relationship, it's a big mistake. It's the same as telling your boyfriend you LOVE football, camping, fishing, and bowling (Not to mention beer and fried food); then once the ring is on your finger-football is boring and confusing, camping a chore, fishing is disgusting and bowling sucks. So what I am saying is that if you didn't like the sex 'for real', get horny and totally crave his body-it was all a big ruse. And somewhere in your past you never got to experience good sex. I feel that good sex happens in an atmosphere where the desire to be close and intimate prevails. You have to be SELFISH in sex-if the sex is bad, it's the woman's fault at least 50% of the time.

Excuses For Loss Of Passion:

1. exhausted

2. depressed

3. crummy periods-too often, painful, etc.

4. he stops paying enough attention to you and vice versa

5. snoring

6. withholding sex as a punishment

7. the kids will hear us

These are all 'excuses' and not valid reasons, but we give them anyway. My answers to the above problems are:

* You have to want sex for yourself and it's inherent pleasure.

* You have to want a well-rounded relationship.

* You have to TRUST your partner.

The Ultimate Fantasy- To accomplish these principles, here's a scenario that has been wildly successful for me:Call your partner during the day while assuming the role of a complete stranger. Invite him to your home (if you're married it's naturally both your homes) for a 'huge surprise.' Greet him at the door, speaking softly and sexily. Touch him gently-act as you would with a stranger-a bit hesitantly and coyly. Ask him about his day and get him to talk about himself-men do this so well!!

The Play-Have the candles lit and sexy music playing in the background. Dinner should be ready but on hold, so the good smells permeate the air. Lead him gingerly to the bedroom or couch. Take off his tie-or whatever-just one thing will get his motor running. Take off your out-erwear to reveal a sexy undergarment. Then, do your thing-but remember he is a STRANGER.

After you have been satisfied (ladies first) and you have made him quiver in ecstasy, get up and go to another room and get dressed. Then when you come back (this is critical) go about your business and pretend the encounter never happened. Never even speak of it. Both of you will love it! A 'timid' woman can do things in a role she might be too inhibited to do as 'herself'.

Regards,

Jeri

* * * MY ANALYSIS * * *

Whew! Were you squirming in your seat?? Are you ready to assume a persona and try this one on your man? Sounds like a great time to me! I chose this particular letter because it addressed several of the same issues brought up in previous chapters. She voiced a definite opinion on the question of whether women *audition* for sex before marriage.

1. She felt that in many instances, women do audition. And she feels they do it because they never learned how to respond sexually in the first place. So to her, it was dishonest *play acting* for the man. Women, especially in her generation, never had the sexual freedom and resources available to take responsibility for their own sexuality. So they learned to become *great fakers* to please their men because that is what was expected of them.

The answer to this dilemma is that *women must take responsibility for their own sexual education and sexual responses.* We should not believe that it is up to the man to *teach us* or hope that it will *come naturally.* And once you learn how to become orgasmic through practicing masturbation or whatever technique you study, your body will become conditioned to respond every time. Then it's your responsibility to get your partner to elicit that response from you. You can tell him what feels great, move your body into a position that turns you on, and build up to the moment of orgasm by utilizing creative foreplay. But now your body has learned that response and it's something that it doesn't *forget.* You will be able to achieve orgasm every time during sex when you become responsible for it. Assuming that females take longer to reach an orgasmic state than males, it is also under your control to make sure you have one before he does, unless you can manage to do it simultaneously. You can orchestrate and elicit the response you want from his stimulus, but the orgasm belongs to YOU!

2. The second thing she illustrated was the importance of role playing for women who are somewhat inhibited about their own sexuality. Playing the *stranger* was her ticket to expressing sexual freedom without feeling uncomfortable. Sometimes you feel a lot more aggressive and experimental when you are not being *yourself.* When there are too many inhibitions attached to the old self, just become a *new woman.* And it is so important that you know that this is PERFECTLY ALL RIGHT to do. You are both consenting adults, enjoying your sexuality. This particular scenario may not be your *cup of tea,* but find one or several that work for you. Think about a particular movie or novel that really turned you on. Then re–enact it in your own personalized fashion. You will be amazed at the depth of your own responses. And once you see how incredibly capable you are of response, it will build your confidence like nothing else can.

WHY PASSION SUBSIDES IN A RELATIONSHIP

This letter was written by Susan, a divorced woman in her mid–thirties who was, unfortunately, the recipient of ongoing marital infidelity. But fortunately, she has moved on to a fulfilling life and a new love. The lessons she learned from her unfortunate marital experience were turned into positives, and she gained substantial wisdom from doing so. It is very uplifting to hear the wisdom of women who have moved on successfully without getting stuck in the patterns of bitterness and revenge, which could have ultimately ruined the lives they have left. This woman began by listing the issues that she feels are responsible for squeezing the passion out of a relationship:

```
Dear Jan,

Here are a few problem areas which I feel contribute to a
loss of passion in a relationship:

1. Children-interference, and always being interrupted

2. Hobbies-Get too busy, spend too much money, then resent-
   ment builds up

3. Preoccupation-trying to achieve materialistic goals at
   the expense of the relationship

4. Full Households-relatives, live-ins, kids

5. Stress-medical problems, work, school, etc

Can You Get The Passion Back? Absolutely!-It takes work,
time and energy, but it's possible through open communica-
tion, playfulness and allowing yourself to be vulnerable
again.

1. Have A Date Night-Just the two of you-alternate who sur-
   prises who-share the responsibility of planning it.

2. Give Cards-Take a few minutes out of the day to sur-
   prise each other with a love note or card. It will put
   a smile on your face and in your heart.

3. Flowers-Both the man and woman should give flowers for
   NO reason. Surprises are the best.

4. Romantic Dinner With Candlelight-Play soft, sexy music
   and DANCE together! Lots of kissing, hugging, and touch-
   ing. Don't ever be shy about touching one another all
   the time.

5. Get A Babysitter-Or plan a sleepover for the kids and
   book a room at your favorite nearby hotel. Buy him a
   gift. Buy yourself something sexy from Victoria's
   Secret.

6. Call Him At Work-Arrange to pick him up and take him to
   a hotel and RAVAGE him! He will absolutely adore this!

7. Be Creative-Take the boredom out of the bedroom and thus
```

the relationship.

8. Play Dress Up-Act out your fantasies. Be a lion tamer,belly dancer, cowgirl or a stripper- just to mention a few possibilities.

9. Play Together-Have a pillow fight, bike together, or whatever else you find is fun.

10. Keep Yourself Looking Good-Work out and look sexy. Or dress up for him for no special reason, then let him UNDRESS you.

11. Ask Him What HIS Needs Are-We always seem to be so busy trying to get our own needs met, it's important to care about this.

12. Have Phone Sex-Do it when he's away on business or out of town for a few days.

13. Accept Each Other As You Are-It's a mistake to try to change someone.

14. Keep Learning Together-Watch less TV and take a class together or read together. This will allow you to grow and always have stimulating conversation together.

15. Be Respectful-Give each other the acknowledgement you both deserve.

Passion In Your Life Starts With You-Passion is a way of living and affects everything you do and will naturally extend to your partner in forms of nurturing. It will allow your relationship to grow and expand dynamically. But passion starts with yourself. You need to do something differently or change your routine to spark a little excitement in your own life. If one has the desire to bring back passion into their relationship, it takes will power and the necessary exploration to achieve that goal. But it starts with you first.Look at your loved one or think about him with new eyes. Thinking of your loved one should bring joy to your life, put a smile on your face and add a lightness to your outlook. Work at keeping anger, resentfulness, frustration and stress out of your relationship. These are all self-defeating attitudes which have no place in a healthy relationship.

Love,

Susan

* * * *ANALYZING WHAT SHE SAID* * * *

Susan's letter was so positive and filled with such wisdom! The one thing that struck me about her whole philosophy is that she operates from a strong position of selflessness. Most of her comments were directed at making the other person happy. She puts this principle into action every-day in her relationship: The more you do for another, the more they want to give back to you. And it's obviously working beautifully in her present relationship. Her whole demeanor is one of rising above problems by giving of herself.

The second thing that struck me was that she feels very strongly about fulfilling yourself before you can fulfill another. What she's saying is it's important to come to the other person WHOLE and FULFILLED. Don't be a half-empty cup and then expect the other person to fill you up. If we enter a relationship out of extreme need and unfulfillment, we will place unrealistic expectations on the other person. And of course, they can't ful-fill all your expectations. NO ONE CAN. So the relationship is doomed from the outset because the unfulfilled person feels constantly disappoint-ed in the other person for not providing that to him. This is not to say that we can't learn from our partner, grow together or nurture each other. That's what a relationship is all about. But we have a responsibility to make our-selves as complete as possible through education, utilizing our talents and creativity and hard work. The more you bring into the relationship, the more you are going to get out of it.

—WEDNESDAY DATE NIGHT—

Helene has been happily married for 12 years. She and her husband are still "lovers" as well as "buddies:"

Dear Jan,

Every Wednesday night since we got married has been our designated 'date night.' We dress up and go out alone to a place that we know will delight the other. One week he plans it, the next time I plan it. And we make it a surprise for each other. Over the years we have become very creative in what we plan. We've done moonlight picnics at the beach, romantic restaurants, an evening at a hotel and hot dogs at the pier. But no matter where we go, we always shower and spruce up for our night together. We also always end our 'date' by coming home and making glorious love.

Even after our kids came, we never stopped this ritual. Oh, maybe for a few weeks after they were born, but that's about it. I always planned for the sitter and to this day I still do. This practice has kept our romance alive and our passion cooking. It's our way of proving to each other that marriage did not end our romance and the ability to keep each other a top priority. It's been the single most effective tool I can think of that has kept us so close throughout our marriage. And we plan on doing this until we're at least 90!

Love,

Helene

THE IMPORTANCE OF DATING

What they have done, exemplifies the principle of prioritizing time for each other into long-term action. You can imagine that this is not always the easiest thing in the world to accomplish week after week for 12 years. But they have done it because it was really important for them to maintain a romantic atmosphere in their marriage. They have successfully proven that romance doesn't ever have to end in a relationship if you don't want it to.

Her letter illustrates the point beautifully that *working* at a relationship shouldn't be equated with drudgery and doing things you'd rather not have to do. On the contrary, if we can adopt the attitude that *working for* the relationship can be accomplished in pleasurable and fun ways, it changes our perspective. Scheduling romantic dates, playing together and affirming one another are all positive and fun things to do. Let's get rid of that old term *working at the relationship* and replace it with *creating pleasure in the relationship*. It's a more accurate and positive term which allows us to become more excited about the whole concept.

CHAPTER 11

PRACTICAL SUGGESTIONS

TIPS FOR IMPLEMENTING WHAT YOU HAVE LEARNED

We women are by nature very practical beings. We are open to learning theory, but also need concrete advice about how to put what we have learned into practice. This chapter will give you some tips and techniques for doing just that.

* * * ARGUMENTS AND COMMUNICATION * * *

1. TAPE YOUR ARGUMENTS AND DISCUSSIONS – If you find that you are arguing much too frequently or your discussions invariably escalate into big fights every time you have them, tape one or several of them. You may have to buy one of those portable taping units, but it's a small investment considering the amount of emotional damage inflicted on both of you from continual and vitriolic fighting. Granted, you won't always know when you're about to have a fight, but you can start out by taping one of your discussions. Play it back and really listen to your dialogue. Keep a keen and analytical ear out for all those trouble spots we discussed in previous chapters. Listen to see if you were being critical, nagging or hostile. Were you getting off track and arguing about everything but the issues? Listen for key words or phrases that were responsible for escalating the discussion into a full-blown fight. Play it for your husband too, so you can both take responsibility for the things you actually said that were out of line. This also helps to clarify certain points, if you both remember things differently after the discussion. You can go back and see if one of you is consciously or unconsciously misconstruing the facts and wrongly accusing the other. When you do this, it's going to be a real *eye-opener*. You will find that it's a very useful tool in helping you to avoid the same old patterns over and over again.

2. WRITE DOWN THE KEY POINTS OF THE CHAPTER ON ARGUMENTS–List the trouble spots like interrupting, shouting, blaming, etc. and check off the ones you're guilty of doing. And when you have your next discussion or fight, remember them and make a conscious effort to stop using them. Every time you eliminate one of these negative ways of

communicating, put a star next to it on your list. Continue this practice until you have eliminated most of these negative responses.

This is a sample of the checklist you might formulate and use to check off the infractions you are guilty of during arguments:

1. Nagging
2. Continued Screaming Without Taking A Time-Out
3. Using Manipulation
4. Bringing Unrelated Problems Into The Argument
5. Not Apologizing When You Know You're In The Wrong
6. Sarcasm
7. Employing Revenge Tactics
8. Screaming, Shouting, Nasty Inflections
9. Foul Language
10. Invalidating The Other's Opinions
11. Personal Attacks
12. Constantly Interrupting
13. Resorting To Silence
14. Issuing Ultimatums
15. Threatening To Leave

3. ESTABLISH A "TIME-OUT" POLICY – When you see that your argument is going nowhere because tempers are flaring or you are both not sticking to the issue, then just stop for a specified period of time. Agree to come back together after you both cool down and can resume being more analytical in discussing the problem. Make it a policy to stop wasting your time getting trapped in arguments that go nowhere. Your time is better spent doing ANYTHING else but that.

4. ALLOW 5 MINUTES FOR EACH PARTY TO EXPRESS HIS OPINION – Each party should have a 3-5 minute time limit to express his point of view WITHOUT INTERRUPTION from the other. This makes it easier to really listen to the other's feelings and allow them to express the whole story before responding. It will eliminate the tendency for either party to attempt to dissect each and every point along the way.

5. SET A TIMER FOR 15 MINUTES – If you go beyond it, take a time out. Or, if you are really close to wrapping it up, do so. Too much valuable time is taken up by repeating the same points over and over. Besides, they lose all their effectiveness when you keep repeating them. Learning to keep it short is a very positive tool in helping to focus your thoughts and keep-

ing your comments succinct.

6. THREATS ARE OFF-LIMITS – Make a rule between you that no matter how heated the argument gets, you will never threaten to leave the house, each other or the marriage. This is one of the worst tactics you can use in an argument. It's playing dirty. Threats will serve only to stifle any hope of resolution and make both of you unwilling to discuss any further matters.

7. DON'T CARRY A GRUDGE – If you do, it means the argument wasn't resolved to your satisfaction. Discuss it again. However, you must always take responsibility for your part in any discussion. If you did something wrong, it's up to you to apologize. If you have both agreed the argument is over, then learn to forgive him and yourself. The person who holds a grudge will find that it constantly eats them up inside. So, if you are guilty of it, make a concerted effort to rid yourself of this behavior.

8. DIG DEEPER – Even if your mate has said or done something which angers you to the point of wanting to scream at him–don't. Force yourself to dig deeper and uncover what's beneath your anger. Say to yourself, "I'm angry because.........and this makes me afraid because.........and fill it in honestly. Then voice your FEARS to him which are underlying your anger. Practice this during all your discussions until you can zero in on what's REALLY bothering you. It will keep your arguments shorter and to a large extent, take the vitriolic out of them.

9. ESTABLISH AN ARENA OF TRUST –Whenever two people voice differing opinions, it's important that you both come from a solid basis of trust between you. This is accomplished when you enter the disagreement KNOWING THAT NO MATTER WHAT THE DIFFERENCES ARE, THE OTHER PERSON HAS YOUR BEST INTERESTS AT HEART. When this atmosphere is prevalent, it takes a lot of the animosity out of the basic disagreement. Both parties must be in agreement that they are not to invalidate each other, but work together towards finding a resolution.

Trust means love and the expression of that love without manipulation. When strings are attached to caring and love, this is called "manipulation" and has no place in the relationship. So both parties need to make a conscious effort to be honest and straightforward when discussing any issue. And every time you do this, you will help build and maintain the trust between you.

These topics are an abridged recap of what was covered in our discussions about arguing and communication. However, no one's situation is exactly like another's. Just becoming aware of the problem is always the first step in taking positive action to correct it.

The chapter following the communication section dealt with the problem of children and how couples advertently or inadvertently allow them to dampen the passion and romance in their marriages. The following section will give you some concrete suggestions about how to provide you and your spouse with the necessary *alone time* that will keep your relationship nurtured and romantic.

* * * *THE KIDS* * * *

1. MAKE IT A PRIORITY TO SEARCH FOR COMPETENT SITTERS – If you have a baby or very young children and are reluctant to leave them with just any babysitter, call a nurses' dormitory and ask if they have a list of students who are looking for babysitting jobs. I did this when my kids were very young and it worked out great. I interviewed several and chose a few who were trustworthy and needed the work. Student nurses are usually always happy to sit, need the money and have experience with babies and children of all ages. This also works with camp counselors, graduate students or college students. It's well worth your time to do a little investigating. You'll end up with very reliable sitters and your mind will be at ease when you go out.

2. DO A SWAP WITH YOUR FRIENDS – Call a girlfriend who has kids approximately the same age, and arrange a swap on the weekend. Your child spends a Friday night at your friend's house and you take her child on the Saturday night. This can be arranged in any combination of ways which suit both your needs. It saves money, frees up an entire evening for closeness with your mate and the kids love spending the night with their friends!

3. TAKE ADVANTAGE OF "KIDS CAMPS" – When you want to get away for the weekend and can't get a sitter, many of the bigger hotels have a "Kids Camp" in conjunction with their other services. For example, if you are on a ski trip and the kids are too young to ski or don't want to, many hotels offer an all-day camp with fun activities for kids of all ages. Many stay open until 10 PM which gives you the whole day for your adult activities. And they don't cost an arm and a leg, either. Call ahead and ask if they offer this program and find out how much they charge. It's a wonderful solution for everyone.

4. MOM AND DAD TIME – Start teaching your kids at a very young age that Mommy and Daddy have their *special times* together when they are not to be interrupted. Then set aside that time and share it together just being close. Do not bring up negative topics. Use it for positives only to show your continued support of one another. Children are a lot more flexible than you think. If you start this practice while they are very young, they will soon understand the importance it has for everyone in the family.

5. SPREAD YOUR UNCONDITIONAL LOVE AROUND–All of us Moms love our kids unconditionally. It's a natural way in which we express our love. But be GENEROUS with those feelings and remember to always extend them to your spouse too. Always approach him positively, by giving him the same benefit of the doubt as you would your kids. If he apologizes for something he did that upset you, accept his apology graciously. This approach will do wonders to maintain a loving, harmonious climate between you. Take the time to write a list of all the things you really love and appreciate about him. Read it once a week and add to it. Make a habit of living in this positive atmosphere. When you do this regularly, it will alleviate tensions and help make any future arguments a lot less hostile than they used to be.

The next subject we discussed was sex and passion in your relationship. The following topics are highlights from that chapter which offer specific advice for better lovemaking.

* * * SEX * * *

1. DON'T GIVE "ORDERS" DURING LOVEMAKING–It's important to ask for what you want in bed from your partner, but avoid acting like *the director* and giving him *orders*. This means keeping the instructional tone out of your voice. When you constantly say things like, "a little more here, not so hard, touch me here" and other non-stop instructions, it's going to cause a major negative impact on your partner. He will end up feeling controlled, pressured and worst of all, like he's a lousy lover who doesn't know what he's doing. So do some talking BEFORE you actually make love, which will open up the communication about what you want. Then when you're making love, allow him the freedom of exploring and touching without being constantly directed. It won't take him long to discover which moves really turn you on by your movements, moans of pleasure and responsiveness.

2. IT'S OK TO BE SELFISH IN BED–If you are always concerned about giving pleasure to your man and not really interested in getting any for yourself, it's not normal. This behavior indicates a big problem with your self-esteem. It says that you don't think you are good enough as a wife or lover. Remember that sex is supposed to give pleasure and act as a release for BOTH parties. You are entitled to the same pleasures and sensual feelings as your partner. So go ahead and take the time you need to become fully aroused by your partner. This takes a complete knowledge of your own body and the specific areas which need to be stimulated for your arousal. And if you reach an orgasm first, it's perfectly all right. There is nothing written in stone which says you have to achieve a simultaneous orgasm every time you have sex.

3. JUST DO IT–Quit putting off sex with a variety of excuses and get back into the practice of JUST DOING IT. We discussed a variety of reasons why women get into the habit of avoiding sex in previous chapters. But another reason you should consider, which might be behind your sexual avoidance, is the fear of intimacy. Many people are afraid of ultimately being rejected and of the hurt they will sustain. This goes for both sexes. To help overcome the fear of intimacy, just hold and caress one another while verbalizing how much you love, need and cherish each other. Do this for a week or two without actually having intercourse until you feel safe and comfortable. Slowly, your mind and body will begin to re-open to the idea of sexual intimacy again. And when you feel secure and loving enough, just let it happen. But once it's re–established, don't ever allow yourself to get back into the avoidance mode again. Always remember that men, especially, need to have sex in order to feel wanted. A sexual rejection for any reason will be taken as a personal one in many cases. So keep that in mind when you re-think your entire sexual role in the marriage.

4. THINK MORE LIKE A MAN–Men like women who like sex. They don't want to spend all their time coaxing or begging for sex. They see it as a normal, healthy and pleasurable function–which it is! And women should see it this way, too. Educate yourself sexually in the ways we talked about in previous chapters. Delight in the fact that *you are a sexual woman of the 90's*. Lose those archaic ideas about sexy women being *sluts* or *tramps*. If you still think this way, you've got a lot of remedial work to do on yourself. Sex is beautiful, healthy and the core factor in keeping every marriage passionate. It's your RIGHT to have it this way.

5. MAKE KISSING A PRIORITY–Get into the habit of giving long kisses once a day–at least. This is going to be kissing that does not lead to sex. It will be for other reasons. It helps you get more connected with each

other by re-establishing those old romantic feelings of being *crazy* about each other. Do it before work, when he gets home or even before breakfast. Learn to *go with* it and not worry about other things you could be doing. Just melt in his arms like you used to and bask in the comfort of being held and adored.

6. ESTABLISH YOUR DATE NIGHT–Set one night aside for you and your husband to go out alone. Go dancing, dining or whatever you want–but make it a priority in your lives from now on. Don't let anything interfere with it, because it's going to work miracles for both of you! Also, make plans to "get away" one weekend a month alone. You can also achieve this by having your home to yourselves on a particular evening. This will be your time to re-build your romance together. Don't ever feel guilty about giving yourselves that time. You deserve it for yourselves and your relationship!

The following is a piece of advice which you should keep in mind when forming friendships as a part of your socialization as a couple. It is very important for a couple to live in as positive an atmosphere as possible by surrounding themselves with friends who have stable and happy relationships.

* * * SURROUND YOURSELVES WITH HAPPILY MARRIED COUPLES * * *

When you look for a job, you wouldn't want to accept one that has a workplace with a negative or depressing aura. The same should apply to the atmosphere for your relationship. Make it a practice to have friends who are happily married or committed couples. There is nothing more enlightening or uplifting than to be around people who practice making their marriages happy and romantic. We can learn a lot from observing their interactions and applying it to our own relationships. It establishes a positive atmosphere for us to continue working on our own relationships and a source to keep learning from.

And even though we women often counsel other women and support them a great deal in their life's problems, it's a good idea to keep a balance for the sake of our own emotional equanimity. A woman who spends hours every day listening to their girlfriends relate depressing or angry stories about their divorces or cheating husbands, can't help but let some of the negativity rub off on themselves and the way they think about their own relationships. So it makes good sense to maintain a balance in these matters by having most of your relationships with happily married couples. We have choices as to who we spend our time with and what we do with our lives. Let's get smart and fill them up with as many positives as possible.

* * * * * *

The following pages contain a cut-out section
for your HUSBAND or SIGNIFICANT OTHER.
It contains suggested ways in which he can help you
both in your quest for more romance and
passion in your relationship.

SUGGESTIONS FOR THE MEN

Your wife/partner bought this book because she is seriously committed to reviving some of the passion and intimacy in your relationship. And the goal of this book is to help you BOTH get back the intense feelings of romance and passion you enjoyed when you were beginning your relationship or you had in the first few years of marriage. She is going to work on improving the communication skills between you and needs your help in doing so. It is her goal that she will become a more loving, more attentive and sexier partner. And I'm sure you'll find no objection to any of those things!

It would also greatly benefit you to read this book. However, we gals are REALISTS and know that our chances of getting you to read it cover to cover are slim and none. Right?? So, as a realistic author, I have solved the problem for you. I've included this cut-out section with a list of the points I feel men need to know in order to better help your partner achieve her goals for both of you. It's so much easier to avoid those old traps when you understand where she is coming from emotionally and intellectually. And once you do, you can move ahead and give her your cooperation in helping her minimize those trouble spots or eradicate them altogether.

The topics and behavioral techniques I am relating to you have already been read by your partner in the previous chapters. I have given her the same advice for her actions and behavior that I am giving you. In this section, I have listed some topics, which I feel men need to fully understand, and have made suggestions about how you can begin improving them. In combination with your wife's efforts, you will both be practicing some very powerful techniques which will help restore the love and trust in your relationship. And this will result in helping you both to re-build intimacy and passion which ultimately translates into better and hotter sex for both of you.

* * * SUGGESTIONS FOR BETTER COMMUNICATION * * *

1. MAKE A "TIME OUT" POLICY – Both men and women know from experience that their arguments often get heated to the point where the main issues are lost in a blur of anger. At this point, it's futile to go on because both sexes have SHUT DOWN to suggestions and really aren't listening to the other anymore. When this happens, it's very important for both of you to just STOP and take a time out. We make our kids do this and we need to follow our own advice. So stop and agree to come back together in 15 minutes, an hour or the next day—whatever you both think best. Cool down. Let your anger subside. I guarantee that you will be a lot more focused and clear-headed when you resume your discussion. And of course, your goal is to solve the problem and not to just stir up needless bad feelings between you. This technique has been proven to work in countless relationships.

2. DON'T UNLEASH YOUR ANGER AT YOUR PARTNER – Okay, this is one of those subjects that may seem a bit unfair to the men at first. However, you have got to understand that when you show anger towards your woman, it really SCARES her. She will either shut down or begin screaming back at you because her fear makes it very hard to deal with you rationally. Women cannot handle men's anger. They are used to being protected by men. So it's one of those things that will build a wall between you faster than anything else. So please, when the anger bubbles up and you feel the urge to shout at your wife, just step back. Tell her you are going to your den or your workshop to cool off and regain your self-control. I have asked women to do the same. But you have to understand that a woman's anger doesn't THREATEN a man like a man's anger threatens a woman. Men are much more accustomed to aggression and handle it better than women do. So for the sake of your future communication and ability to stay close and connected, learn to control your aggression with your woman. It will be of immense benefit to both of you in the long run.

3. LEARN TO APOLOGIZE – Saying "I'm sorry" is one of the most healing things you can do during an argument. We women are strange birds in a lot of ways, I'll admit. Often the easiest and quickest way to end an argument and be forgiven is simply to tell her that you're sorry. But you have to mean it! Many times your spouse will keep an argument going on and on because that's what she is waiting to hear. Too often both sides get bogged down in excuses or lengthy explanations in attempting to validate their own point of view. So when she is really feeling threatened by your anger or by whatever happened, just remember how much you love her and that you don't want her to be hurt. Saying "I'm sorry Honey" will be music to her ears. First of all, it establishes the fact that you love her and take responsibility that you made a mistake. Secondly, it often ends the argument right there. Once she's reassured of your love, there's really not much else she can say.

4. DON'T USE ISOLATION AS YOUR DEFENSE – Men are more likely to go into the *silent treatment* for days or weeks than women. And there are many reasons why. One is that they just get fed up with what they perceive as constant criticisms of them. Another, is that they feel they aren't being listened to by their spouses. And other times, men feel they are being unjustly accused of something. However, even if some of these reasons are valid, your total silence will get you nowhere but into a state of deeper resentment on both sides. The silence will be interpreted as your not caring, a total disregard for her feelings or unwillingness to resolve the problem. And it will eventually wipe out any remaining hope of communication between you and permanently damage your relationship. It will also kill your sex life and the passion between you.

5. LEARN TO COMPROMISE – Whenever you have two points of view being discussed, more likely than not, neither person is going to get his own way 100% of the time. And this often gets interpreted as one person *losing* and the other *winning* the argument. It also makes arguments drag on and on until one person *gives in* to the other's wishes. I have already discussed this with your wife and have given her the same advice–learn to COMPROMISE on issues. *Men are by nature better problem solvers than women.* They see things less emotionally which allows them to have a better understanding of evaluating a problem in terms of possible compromise. When you compromise, you should both feel like you've *gained something* for the good of your relationship rather than *giving up* your own point of view. THIS IS CONSIDERED A WIN-WIN SITUATION.

For example: If you want to play poker on a certain night and your wife wants you home to do something for her, figure out a way to do both. You may promise to do it at a later date or come home early to help her–whatever you can work out between you. By doing this, she won't feel like you are *choosing* to be with the guys over being with her. And underneath it all, this is really what's bothering her.

6. NEVER ATTEMPT TO END AN ARGUMENT BY ISSUING AN ULTIMATUM – The whole point of having a discussion about any topic is to arrive at some meeting of the minds on it. When one partner issues an ultimatum by saying "It's my way or else" that shows a complete lack of willingness to compromise on any level. There may be times when your wife may come around to your way of thinking or vice–versa. But it has to be done out of her own free will. Ultimatums are the tactics of a bully and will bring about seething resentment from

149

your partner. Relationships are strengthened by acts of compromise but ultimatums destroy them.

* * * SEX * * *

1. EXTEND YOUR FOREPLAY TIME – In general, men and women come from totally different points of view about sex. For women, sex happens in their minds first before it gets translated into body stimulation. But men are much more physically oriented. So I am telling you straight out that your woman needs more tenderness, romance and extended foreplay to "heat her up" than you probably realize. Don't go straight to her genitals or breasts when you begin making love. Most women feel a sense of being invaded when a man reaches for these parts before arousing her with more indirect foreplay. And don't take it as a PERSONAL REJECTION if she's not "rarin' to go" after five minutes. ALL WOMEN need more time than that to fully respond. We are all anatomically the same and require a lot of stimulation coupled with a sense of being loved before our brains will signal our genitals to become aroused. It's just a fact of female anatomy. And when you men really begin to understand this concept and act accordingly, you will find that your sex life will improve dramatically. Women require the "emotional stroking" as well as the physical stroking to get their engines running!

2. REMEMBER: ANGER SHUTS WOMEN OFF TO SEX– When your wife is angry at you, it's the WORST time to approach her for sex. You're going to meet with rejection 9 times out of 10. So don't put both of you through it. Settle the problem with her first AND THEN give her lots of loving reassurance that everything is okay between you. It takes women a lot longer to bounce back from emotional upsets than men. This is another one of those "differences between the sexes" principles. And when you really get it, you'll be able to deal with it properly to attain the results you want. So don't fight it. Make sure the argument is completely resolved to both your satisfactions and no residual hostility remains. Then reassure her that your love is still as strong as ever.

3. BOLSTER YOUR WOMAN'S SEXUAL IMAGE OF HER-SELF – Many women have a very poor sexual image of themselves. They are over-critical of their bodies and have forgotten how to feel and act sexy. So it's most important for a husband to give his constant approval to her so that she can regain a better image of herself. I know that many men try to do this for their wives and feel it has no results. But it does. It's just that women need CONTINUAL reassurance. So don't feel like your efforts are in vain, believe me, they aren't. I've given your woman a lot of suggestions in the book on how to improve her sexual image and her sexuality. But she will need your positive input on a continuing basis to help her achieve her goal.

4. TALK TO HER IN BED – Another one of the most common complaints I hear from women is about their husbands' lack of verbal assurance in bed. They hate it when a man remains silent when making love, then finishes and rolls over to sleep. I know you've all heard that scenario a million times before, but it's all too often the truth. More than anything else, your wife wants you to talk to her DURING SEX and AFTER SEX. It doesn't mean that you need to keep up a real dialogue in bed, but she does want to hear how much she's loved, cherished and how beautiful she looks in your eyes. Believe me, this will do more to turn her on and get her body to become receptive than an hour of silent foreplay. Always remember that sex for your woman, begins and ends in HER HEAD. And even though it is indeed a lot more of a physical phenomenon for you as a man, you are not doing it by yourself! You will need to understand what turns HER on, in order to get the MOST out of sex for BOTH of you.

5. GO SLOWLY – When either of you pays too much immediate attention to the genitals without letting your sexual energy build up throughout your entire body, it can result in premature ejaculation in the male or a premature orgasm in the woman. Be aware of how fast you are moving. Learn to slow yourself down by talking or just holding each other or by regulating your breathing. Let that sexual tension build up slowly and completely for both of you. Your orgasms will be more powerful and your satisfaction and fulfillment much more complete when you allow yourself the time it takes to slowly build to that peak of pleasure and release.

6. ROMANCE HER ALL DAY: NOT JUST WHEN YOU WANT TO HAVE SEX – If I've heard it once, I've heard it a thousand times from women–the art of making love begins long before you hit the sheets! They CANNOT be all business one minute and go into immediate heat when they get into bed with you! They want to be romanced a little while you're watching TV or just sitting on the couch together. You have to set the stage on your lovemaking nights. Tell her you love her, hold her hand and kiss her neck during the evening.

Then, she'll be much more receptive to your touch and sexual advances when you get into bed hours later. And when you practice this kind of romancing all the time and not just as a preparation for sex, you'll find that she's a lot more willing to have sex "spontaneously" than ever before. Start thinking of your entire relationship as "one big foreplay". This is what your woman has been wanting all her life.

* * * HELPING HER BUILD BETTER SELF-ESTEEM * * *

1. DON'T NAG HER ABOUT HER WEIGHT – Many women become sexually apathetic, display more jealousy, and feel the relationship is threatened when they think they're unattractive because they are overweight. I have discussed this in a previous chapter with your wife and have given her guidance and motivation to get on a weight reduction program right away, if she feels that her weight is causing self-esteem problems. You can help immensely by encouraging her, once she has begun her program. But nagging her will not give her the motivation to start one. It has to come from WITHIN her and she has to motivate herself.

Once she has begun her program, you can add to her motivation by acting as her biggest "cheerleader" and by telling her things of this nature:

- "I notice you're looking trimmer."
- "I'll buy you a sexy teddy when you lose your first five pounds."
- "You look so sexy in that bathing suit."
- "I'm so happy to see that you are doing something positive for yourself and your health."
- "I'm really pleased that you are feeling so much happier and secure about yourself."

2. ENCOURAGE HER IN HER INTELLECTUAL PURSUITS – Your partner might be lacking in self-esteem because she feels intellectually inferior to you or the people she associates with. And when she feels this way about herself, she tends to become insecure and defensive in her behavior. I have encouraged your wife (and all women who feel this way about themselves) to enroll in courses which she thinks would help her in certain areas, or to attend some seminars and read more to help her broaden her intellectual scope.

If your wife has decided to do any of these things to better herself, it's important that you understand why she's doing it and encourage her. You might:

- Take a course with her.

- Teach her about areas in which you excel like investments, the computer, or any number of things.

- Don't make her feel guilty about the time she's investing to better her mind–she's not only doing it for herself, but also to make you proud of her.

3. TELL HER OFTEN HOW MUCH YOU APPRECIATE HER EFFORTS FOR YOU AND THE FAMILY – Many women adopt a sullen and negative attitude when they feel that all their efforts to make a happy home go unnoticed. Your wife has already been reminded that it's very important for her to show her appreciation for you and your efforts and contributions as head of your family; so I'm asking you to return the compliment. You can accomplish this in hundreds of small ways, some of which are:

- Compliment her on how hard she works to keep the houseclean.

- Help her out with the kids whenever possible.

- Thank her for doing the laundry or picking up the clothes at the cleaners.

- Tell her what a great job she's doing with the kids.

- Take notice of the extra things she does to keep you happy like preparing your favorite meal or making your dental appointments, etc.

- If she gets sick with a cold or flu, take over some of her responsibilities and give her a lot of T.L.C. until she's better.

- Always remember her birthday and your anniversary properly with a beautiful card and flowers or something really special.

- Make it a point to tell her how pretty she looks even when she's not all "dolled up."

- Tell her how much you love her at least once everyday.

- Show your appreciation at unexpected times by surprising her with a little love note, some flowers or some other small token to let her know how much you love her and how much she means to you.

* * * TRUST * * *

1. KNOW THAT A WOMAN PLACES HER LIFE IN YOUR HANDS – Marriage for your wife means that she has entrusted her life to you. She trusts that you will put her welfare above all else and never hurt her. And it's only after you have earned her complete trust, will she be able to give herself to you emotionally, as well as physically. If that trust is damaged for any reason, you'll find that it will affect every other part of your relationship, especially your sexual interaction. When trust is present, your woman will allow herself to give enormously in sex.

Remember, I've stated previously that sex happens mainly in a woman's head. She needs to trust in the fact that you will be there for her "in sickness and in health 'til death do you part." And when your actions assure her of that on a daily basis, her mind will allow her body to accept and give itself completely to you. It's an age-old truth and the basis for every successful marriage.

2. INFIDELITY WILL RUIN A MARRIAGE – A woman has to believe that you will never betray her. Infidelity is the one thing in a marriage that is nearly impossible to overcome. No matter how hard you both work at repairing the damage, the lingering doubts and shattered trust it incurs will ruin your relationship forever. So never take it lightly. There are men who think that one-night stands or quickie affairs aren't that big of a deal. Well, don't ever get deluded into this kind of thinking. Infidelity is the number-one reason for divorce because it kills all trust in a marriage and often makes any hope for re-building future trust between you impossible.

Also, the act of flirting can severely damage her ability to trust you. Most women believe that there is no such thing as harmless flirting. It's degrading to a woman when her husband is openly ogling and playing up to another woman. It's the same as telling her that she's not worthy of your attention. Never underestimate how defiling and degrading to a woman this behavior can be.

3. BE TRUTHFUL – Your woman needs to feel that she can put her faith in everything you tell her. Your word means everything in life and in your relationship as well. If she can't go to the bank on what you say, it's going to have a profound destructive effect on your relationship. If she catches you in one lie, what's to say that she won't think you're lying about the next thing? Lies have a mushrooming effect. And just as there is no such thing as a "harmless affair", likewise, there is no such thing as a "harmless lie."

Lies, ultimately, will destroy all trust. Of course, it's impossible to get through an entire lifetime without ever telling a lie. We all shade the truth to save a person's feelings or keep them from a bigger hurt at times. But here we're talking about the serious kind of lies which erode trust and breed suspicion.

For example: You tell your wife that you are working an extra hour one evening, but in truth, you spend it having a few drinks at a bar. She calls the office and finds out you aren't there. You come home and she smells liquor on your breath. Now you have to admit you lied to her and try to explain why. Even if what you did was entirely innocent, she might jump to the conclusion that you were at the bar with another woman. So this one lie has set up a cycle where she's not going to trust your word and question everything you tell her in the future.

4. TRUST AND RESPECT ARE NECESSARY FOR GOOD SEX – It is so important for you to recognize how closely trust, respect and sex are connected in your spouse's mind. If your woman doesn't trust you, she'll never respect you. And for most women, if they don't respect a man then a successful sex life with him is impossible. When your wife makes love with you, she has to know in her head and heart that you are the man she trusts above all others. Women are taught that their bodies are sacred and should never be given to a man she can't trust. Men are different. Sometimes they can have great sex with a woman they can't trust or don't respect. But it seldom carries over into a marital situation. Both sexes expect and deserve to know that their partner will never hurt them, degrade them or take advantage of them in any way. These are the kinds of breaches in trust that are irreparable.

* * * RESPECT * * *

1. WHAT WOMEN WANT TO BE RESPECTED FOR – Respect is a sensitive issue for women. Many women feel that a man is automatically given respect just because he is a man and because he has a career. Here's a list of things women told me that they feel they aren't getting the proper respect for:

- the dedication they give in raising their families
- keeping their homes running smoothly
- their intelligence
- giving so much of themselves to others

- their creativity
- their opinions and decisions
- their capacity for giving and receiving love
- their ability to please him in lovemaking

Your wife may not be a powerhouse CEO of some corporation but she certainly deserves the same amount of respect for being the CEO of your family. She works like a dog to try and meet everyone's needs, give them her love and attention, solve their problems, keep them healthy, well fed and happy. And she uses her creativity, her intelligence, her knowledge, her talents and her love to accomplish all these things. So try to acknowledge all her efforts by giving her the respect she deserves in all things. And don't wait until Mother's Day or her birthday to tell her how much you love and respect her. Make it a practice of doing it every day. Your relationship will be so much stronger for it!

2. DON'T TRY TO GAIN RESPECT BY BULLYING – Men are taught to be strong and dominant. They are taught that they must have respect. Unfortunately, many males, especially when growing up, try to establish this status through bullying others. And if they gain some small victories along the way, they retain this behavior into adulthood. The idea of winning someone's respect through fear and intimidation is an ill-conceived one. And this goes doubly in a marriage. Shouting, threatening or acting innately superior with your wife will never earn her respect. You might be successful in making her afraid of you, but this should never be confused with her respecting you.

What are the best ways to gain your wife's respect? It's really simple when it's done in positive ways like:

- Always treating her and others with kindness.
- Be reliable. When you promise her you are going to do something, DO IT. Don't make excuses or put it off. This kind of behavior will constantly disappoint her and will build mistrust against you.
- Don't sit in judgement of everything she does. Try to be as accepting and non-judgmental as possible. She is an adult and must feel that you value her opinions and decisions as one.
- Respect her needs. Women have a strong need to be understood

and feel loved at all times. Don't shrug this need off as a "female idiosyncrasy" or as being silly. She needs to hear how much you love her every day to keep her secure and happy. You will discover that a few kind words go a long way. Try it and I guarantee you will be surprised at how attentive she suddenly becomes.

• Respect her intelligence and give her credit for it. Compliment her on making a good decision or acting wisely in a situation when she deserves it. Women do not like men who consider them to be "overly emotional and brainless." When you tell her how much you admire her for her intelligence, she's going to RESPECT YOU MORE for recognizing and verbalizing it.

3. RESPECT HER NEED FOR SPACE – Your wife is probably so busy raising the family and attending to your needs that she finds she has almost no free time for herself. It is an act of unselfishness and kindness for you to help provide her with some much needed "alone time." Volunteer to watch the kids for an hour so she can go relax in a hot, bubbly tub. Or once a month, take charge of the household for an evening so she can play cards with her girlfriends or some other activity. Believe me, she will be eternally grateful and you will reap the rewards of that gratitude a hundred times over! I have already told your wife that she should extend the same courtesy to you.

Having a little time to ourselves does not mean that we don't want to be with you or we need to get away from you! All of us, male or female, need some alone time to collect our thoughts and center ourselves. Marriage should never mean being shackled together. It is normal and healthy to want some time for ourselves. So, promise each other that one night a week, a month or whatever you will each get an alone time. And you must do it in the spirit of love and willingness and not begrudgingly, or else there is no point to it. Respecting each other's time and privacy is a right that needs to be carried out over the course of your marriage.

* * * SOME PARTING THOUGHTS * * *

I know your wife or partner is very happy and encouraged that you have taken the time and interest to read this section especially written for you. Keep it handy and review it from time to time, to refresh your memory about the topics covered and the suggestions of how to put them into practice. And remember, everything that was suggested to you was also discussed with your wife or partner. Relationships are two way streets in ALL respects and any one of these topics could be summed up by the Golden Rule: "Do unto others as you would have them do unto you."

When you and your partner make respect, trust, kindness and courtesy a part of the way you treat each other on a daily basis, then your love and passion will grow as a result. Great sex is not just a matter of having a big orgasm. Great sex comes as a result of practicing all the things we talked about with renewed commitment throughout every day of your lives together. I hope you have gained some insights from this section about how your woman feels and operates in your relationship and you will use this knowledge in making some adjustments in your attitudes, as well as your actions, which will help both of you grow closer emotionally. And the closer you become emotionally, the stronger and more passionate your physical bond will become. Always remember that for your woman, sex happens in her MIND first before it gets passed along as stimuli in her body. When you treat your woman as a precious human being, she'll react like one. Her previous feelings of resentment, self-doubt and unhappiness will slowly begin to disappear. And when this happens, her mind will allow her body to become more responsive, uninhibited and sensual. And this is when you'll both begin to experience the BEST SEX OF YOUR LIVES together. And that sexual bond is one of the strongest forces there is between you in keeping your love, loyalty and passion alive and on fire.

BIBLIOGRAPHY

Barbach, Lonnie G: For Yourself. New York: Signet Books, 1976.

Barbach, Lonnie G: For Each Other. New York: Signet Books, 1982.

Buscaglia, Leo F: Loving Each Other. New York: Fawcett Columbine, 1984.

Copelan, Rachel: 100 Ways To Make Sex Sensational and 100% Safe! Hollywood: Lifetime Books, Inc., 1995.

DeAngelis, Barbara: How To Make Love All The Time. New York: Dell, 1987.

DeAngelis, Barbara: Secrets About Men Every Woman Should Know. New York: Dell, 1990.

Godek, Gregory J.P: Romance 101. Boston: Casablanca Press, Inc., 1993.

Gottman, John: Why Marriages Succeed Or Fail. New York: Simon & Schuster, 1994.

Gray, John: Man, Women and Relationships. Oregon: Beyond Words Publishing, Inc., 1993.

Hunt, Patrick T: Red Hot Monogamy. Los Angeles: CCC Publications, 1994.

Lerner, Harriet G: The Dance Of Anger, New York: Harper & Row Publishers, 1985

Wallerstein, Judith S. and Blakeslee, Sandra: The Good Marriage. New York: Houghton Mifflin Co., 1995.

ABOUT THE AUTHOR

"Ladies, Start Your Engines" is the eleventh book written by national best selling author Jan King. She holds a B.A. in education from the University of Connecticut and an M.A. in Science Education from the University of Pennsylvania. As a relationship expert, she is frequently invited as a guest on national TV talk shows including Leeza, Geraldo, Donahue, Ricki Lake, Montel Williams, Jenny Jones, Rolanda, Jerry Springer, Gabrielle and Lifetime's Biggers and Summers. She has also authored a number of humorous books on womens' issues, including the international bestseller "Hormones From Hell."

She is happily married to her husband Mark and the mother of two sons, Michael and Philip.

TITLES BY CCC PUBLICATIONS

Retail $4.99

"?" book

POSITIVELY PREGNANT

WHY MEN ARE CLUELESS

CAN SEX IMPROVE YOUR GOLF?

THE COMPLETE BOOGER BOOK

FLYING FUNNIES

MARITAL BLISS & OXYMORONS

THE VERY VERY SEXY ADULT DOT-TO-DOT BOOK

THE DEFINITIVE FART BOOK

THE COMPLETE WIMP'S GUIDE TO SEX

THE CAT OWNER'S SHAPE UP MANUAL

PMS CRAZED: TOUCH ME AND I'LL KILL YOU!

RETIRED: LET THE GAMES BEGIN

THE OFFICE FROM HELL

FOOD & SEX

FITNESS FANATICS

YOUNGER MEN ARE BETTER THAN RETIN-A

BUT OSSIFER, IT'S NOT MY FAULT

Retail $4.95

YOU KNOW YOU'RE AN OLD FART WHEN...

1001 WAYS TO PROCRASTINATE

HORMONES FROM HELL II

SHARING THE ROAD WITH IDIOTS

THE GREATEST ANSWERING MACHINE MESSAGES
    OF ALL TIME

WHAT DO WE DO NOW?? (A Guide For New Parents)

HOW TO TALK YOU WAY OUT OF A TRAFFIC TICKET

THE BOTTOM HALF (How To Spot Incompetent
    Professionals)

LIFE'S MOST EMBARRASSING MOMENTS

HOW TO ENTERTAIN PEOPLE YOU HATE

YOUR GUIDE TO CORPORATE SURVIVAL
THE SUPERIOR PERSON'S GUIDE TO EVERYDAY
    IRRITATIONS
GIFTING RIGHT

Retail $5.95
LOVE DAT CAT
CRINKLED 'N' WRINKLED
SIGNS YOU'RE A GOLF ADDICT
SMART COMEBACKS FOR STUPID QUESTIONS
YIKES! IT'S ANOTHER BIRTHDAY
SEX IS A GAME
SEX AND YOUR STARS
SIGNS YOUR SEX LIFE IS DEAD
40 AND HOLDING YOUR OWN
50 AND HOLDING YOUR OWN
MALE BASHING: WOMEN'S FAVORITE PASTIME
THINGS YOU CAN DO WITH A USELESS MAN
MORE THINGS YOU CAN DO WITH A USELESS MAN
THE WORLD'S GREATEST PUT-DOWN LINES
LITTLE INSTRUCTION BOOK OF THE RICH & FAMOUS
WELCOME TO YOUR MIDLIFE CRISIS
GETTING EVEN WITH THE ANSWERING MACHINE
ARE YOU A SPORTS NUT?
MEN ARE PIGS / WOMEN ARE BITCHES
ARE WE DYSFUNCTIONAL YET?
TECHNOLOGY BYTES!
50 WAYS TO HUSTLE YOUR FRIENDS ($5.99)
HORMONES FROM HELL
HUSBANDS FROM HELL
KILLER BRAS & Other Hazards Of The 50's
IT'S BETTER TO BE OVER THE HILL THAN UNDER IT
HOW TO REALLY PARTY!!!

WORK SUCKS!
THE PEOPLE WATCHER'S FIELD GUIDE
THE UNOFFICIAL WOMEN'S DIVORCE GUIDE
THE ABSOLUTE LAST CHANCE DIET BOOK
FOR MEN ONLY (How To Survive Marriage)
THE UGLY TRUTH ABOUT MEN
NEVER A DULL CARD
RED HOT MONOGAMY
    (In Just 60 Seconds A Day) ($6.95)
HOW TO SURVIVE A JEWISH MOTHER ($6.95)
WHY MEN DON'T HAVE A CLUE ($7.99)
LADIES, START YOUR ENGINES! ($7.99)

Retail $3.95
NO HANG-UPS
NO HANG-UPS II
NO HANG-UPS III
HOW TO SUCCEED IN SINGLES BARS
HOW TO GET EVEN WITH YOUR EXES
TOTALLY OUTRAGEOUS BUMPER-SNICKERS ($2.95)

NO HANG-UPS – CASSETTES Retail $4.98
Vol. I: GENERAL MESSAGES (Female)
Vol. I: GENERAL MESSAGES (Male)
Vol. II: BUSINESS MESSAGES (Female)
Vol. II: BUSINESS MESSAGES (Male)
Vol. III: 'R' RATED MESSAGES (Female)
Vol. III: 'R' RATED MESSAGES (Male)
Vol. IV: SOUND EFFECTS ONLY
Vol. V: CELEBRI-TEASE